Elaine Sikorski

COOKING *to the*
IMAGE

A PLATING HANDBOOK

WILEY

Sikorski, Elaine.
  Cooking to the image : a plating handbook / Elaine Sikorski.
    pages cm
  Includes bibliographical references and index.
  ISBN 978-1-118-07597-5 (pbk.)
    1. Food presentation. 2. Table setting and decoration. 3. Cooking—Philosophy. 4. Menus.
I. Title.
  TX740.5.S55 2013
  641.502—dc23

                                                                      2012032313

Printed in the United States of America

V10005370_110118

CONTENTS

1

YOUR FIELD OF VISION ———————————————— 1

2

THE PLATE IN CONTEXT ———————————————— 11

3 FRAMING CULINARY ART ————————————— 22

4 PLATTER TO PLATE: CLASSICAL STYLE ————————— 34

5 PLATE FRAME: NOUVELLE STYLE ————————— 44

PLATE FRAME: NEW AMERICAN STYLE
AND FUSION STYLE _____ **55**

PLATE FRAME: GLOBAL STYLE _____ **67**

8 THE EMERGING MENU:
INTERACTIVE TABLE SETTING ———————— 78

9 DESIGN AND CULINARY PLATE
ARCHETYPES ———————————— 85

10 LOOKING FOR INSPIRATION ———————— 96

PREFACE

Everyone participates in the activities of choosing, preparing, and eating food. People consider such activities in different ways: Food might be perceived as a mundane requirement to fuel a hectic life, or as a celebration in which we connect with nature and art. Food activities can also be experienced as entertainment. Watching a celebrity chef prepare food on TV or looking at images of food brings pleasure to our leisure time.

Images of food have become an important influence in people's lives, but this has not always been the case. For much of recorded history, understanding of food was passed from cook to cook without a picture between them. Cookbooks were written, at first, without any pictures and later with only etchings. Yet, today, the images of food are sometimes more important than the actual food experience. Packaged foods rely on imaging to communicate what is inside the wrapping. Cookbook photographs are sometimes more prominent than recipes. Images, in fact, can be so seductive that we can fail to look beyond the images and see the deeper meanings of food presentations.

Cooking to the Image: A Plating Handbook provides the prerequisites to cultivating a professional viewpoint, to investigating these deeper meanings, by considering the different ways a chef looks at food. Its goal is to provide a map of how a chef creates a plate of food by considering such questions as:

Where in the menu is this food item to be placed?

How will it be served?

How much will it cost?

What food is selected?

How is the food prepared?

How is it presented in relationship to other food on the plate?

This book makes visible the fundamental meanings in plated presentations. Plating exposes a chef's deepest beliefs about what food is, and how food should be. Structured as a design process, *Cooking to the Image: A Plating Handbook* outlines how personal creativity and professional traditions fuse to create successful plated presentations of food.

◎ ABOUT THIS BOOK

Just as a science lab book provides a guide to both scientific knowledge and an understanding of the scientific method, **Cooking to the Image: A Plating Handbook** provides a guide through a chef's methodology. The information and exercises in the book work to unite theory and practice into an organized system for visually expressing flavor. For example, one of the most important exercises guides the cook through a series of re-presentations of the same ingredients to match different style periods of culinary arts. In doing this exercise, not only does the look of the dish change, but the way the flavors are perceived when eating the dish also changes. This, then, leads to an understanding of how presentation affects flavor.

Traditionally, plating is explained as a series of practices that resemble the work of a food stylist. Color, shape, and texture are emphasized as criteria to be evaluated. While recognizing that these practices are useful, it is necessary for a cook to understand how these design elements are part of a *culinary Art history*. The emphasis on certain ingredients, culinary processes, and plating styles all develop from a professional, communal understanding of what food is during different time periods.

Just as Art history has developed as a field of study to contextualize the historical development of artistic styles, this book begins the work of creating a *culinary Art history* by placing plating styles in a professional context. Culinary art periods are framed by menu patterns and service. This *culinary Art history* allows us to see taste presented not only as a means of creating flavor, but also as part of larger professional culture that defines our craft.

Beginning in the seventeenth century, craft began to be considered differently than art. Craft objects are useful; art objects do not have a practical function. This led to the idea that an artist is someone other than a craftsperson—a historical division that often causes a divorce between creativity and technical skill. In contrast, this book's *culinary Art history* shows why technical skill is a necessary part of creativity. In addition, it shows how exquisite technical ability results in what is traditionally called Art. Such a history demonstrates why culinary creativity must be functionally useful to be successful and provides a deeper understanding of the artful craft of cooking.

Organizing visual styles of creating flavor into a *culinary Art history* exposes the cooking theories behind different styles of plate presentations. Understanding theory, in turn, allows for mental preparation prior to achieving mastery of manual skills and provides greater choice and depth in your presentations, once your hands catch up with your head.

Creating Your Plate: A Mental Map

When a professional chef creates a plate, there are multiple considerations that her mind runs through as she narrows her focus. The intended service method, type of menu, and style of food all are filters that affect what foods she will choose, how she will prepare them, and how she will design these choices on the plate. This book is organized around this mental map, which a professional chef navigates almost instinctively. Reading and working through the sections and exercises will allow you to see a plate as a professional chef, and help you understand the necessary steps required to create a successful plate: A plate that will not only look good but also taste good and fit the circumstances of the service. The mental map below diagrams the chapters.

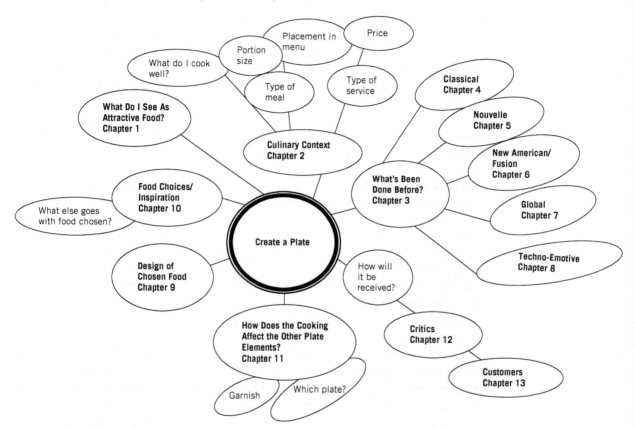

Organization and Approach

Cooking to the Image: A Plating Handbook bridges the divide between teaching kitchens and working kitchens by articulating the theories that are second nature to seasoned professionals. The book introduces the concept of culinary research as an important element in the education of chefs, defining the menu as a central component of culinary understanding. Lastly, the book organizes the artful side of the culinary craft into a *culinary Art history*, so that a diversity of styles can be better appreciated and understood.

While this book can be used to supplement any existing textbook, it pairs especially well with coursework on menu design. **Cooking to the Image: A Plating Handbook** is designed to be a complete course of study focused on culinary creativity, such as a presentation or plating class.

The book is organized into 13 chapters, each ending with a series of Queries and Inquiries. These questions and activities are designed to highlight the key concepts of each chapter and also provide guided instruction in practical applications of the theories presented.

Although each chapter is an independent unit, the chapters are arranged to build plating knowledge in an organic fashion, mirroring the outcomes of years of kitchen practice. This allows the reader to see that no successful plate is ever created outside the parameters of a menu, which define the necessary requisites of the design.

CHAPTER 1: Your Field of Vision describes why an educated viewpoint forms the parameters of plating, explaining that to be able to see something, you first must have a conceptual understanding of what you are looking at: you can't see farther than you can think.

CHAPTER 2: The Plate in Context outlines the guidelines of a chef's vision by relating plate design to a context: the menu. It also provides a framework for culinary research based on menus. Food studies are often considered to be part of scholarly work in fields such as sociology or history; however, as the menu is the working document of a chef, it is also our primary source for culinary research.

CHAPTER 3: Framing Culinary Art introduces an innovative way of considering the visual presentations of food, creating a *culinary Art history*. This new concept fuses the idea of Art history and the traditions of the culinary craft to create Frames defined by menu and service method. These *Frames*, like *periods* within Art history, deepen the understanding of why chefs worked in certain ways and the effects previous culinary work has had, and continues to have, on contemporary culinary styles.

CHAPTERS 4 THROUGH 8, covering **Classical, Nouvelle, New American, Fusion, and Global Styles,** and **Interactive Table Setting**, provide detailed analyses of the styles within the Plate Frame of the *culinary Art history*. Each chapter provides background and guidelines that are the basis of contemporary styles.

CHAPTERS 9 THROUGH 11, covering **Design and Culinary Plate Archetypes, Looking for Inspiration,** and **Plating the Styles**, explore culinary design by relating the various contemporary plate styles to each other. These chapters provide tools to choose, prepare, and associate foods.

CHAPTER 12: Critiquing Culinary Art offers guidance in how to critique a presentation, discussing the values of experts and what can be gained from a well-considered evaluation.

CHAPTER 13: Culinary Values considers the customer's viewpoint by matching different consumer values to the work done by chefs. Furthermore, the craft of cooking is examined in light of changing cultural standards of what constitutes beautiful food.

◎ SUPPLEMENTAL OFFERINGS

A comprehensive online *Instructor's Manual* with *Test Bank* accompanies this book and is available to instructors to help them effectively manage their time and to enhance student learning opportunities.

The *Instructor's Manual* follows an easy-to-use format for each chapter:

A *Chapter Outline* includes the main points of each section within the chapter.

The *Before Class Suggestions* helps instructors organize their lesson plan, providing alternative methods of delivery for each chapter's materials. The instructor may choose classroom, kitchen, or a combination of the two through this section's guided information.

A section of *Kitchen Notes* is provided should instructors decide that a kitchen lab is possible.

A list of *Learning Objectives*, is provided for each chapter, as is a list of *Key Terms and Concepts*.

Discussion Development is an extensive section to help instructors guide discussion. Each chapter's section has points from the text followed by questions. For many of these points, a PowerPoint slide is provided to focus the discussion.

In the *Answers to Queries and Inquires* section, sample answers are provided to the questions and exercises pertaining to the chapter.

The *Test Bank* has been specifically formatted for *Respondus*, an easy-to-use software program for creating and managing exams that can be printed to paper or published directly to Blackboard, WebCT, Desire2Learn, eCollege, ANGEL, and other eLearning systems. Instructors who adopt this book can download the test bank for free.

A password-protected Wiley Instructor Book Companion Web site devoted entirely to this book (www.wiley.com/college/sikorski) provides access to the online *Instructor's Manual* and the text-specific teaching resources. The *Respondus Test Bank* as well as the *PowerPoint* lecture slides are also available on the Web site for download. A list of *Learning Objectives* and *Key Terms and Concepts* are also included on the Instructor and Student Book Companion Web sites.

Elaine Sikorski, C.E.C., C.C.E.

ACKNOWLEDGMENTS

This book emphasizes that to plate successfully, you first must master the craft of cooking before moving on to the art of presentation. To honor this belief, I must first acknowledge my best friend, Marty Attiyeh. Without her mastery of the craft of writing, this book could not have been possible. That simple sentence does not reveal the magnitude of gratitude that I have for Marty because of her help in crafting this manuscript, and even more importantly, over the decades, in crafting my life.

All endeavors and any accomplishments of mine are possible because of the love and support of my family.

The perpetual strength, wisdom, and humor of my mom, Rita Mae Sikorski, my grandmother, Flemmie Ferra, my dad, Ernest Sikorski, and my grandfather, Jerome Ferra are the roots of my successes. Because of what I learned at the kitchen tables of my mom and my grandmother, I am the cook I am today.

My husband, Thierry Tritsch, has given his patience, advice, and support during the creation of this project, as well as all of my other endeavors, which have been essential. His assistance during the photo shoot of this project was invaluable, without which I could not have achieved the results I did. Our daughter, Josephine, has encouraged, comforted, and supported me throughout my struggles with writing. Any achievement on my part is, in part, theirs.

Thank you all, always and forever.

I also want to give a heartful thank you to Jean-Paul Tritsch and Germaine Tritsch for not only accepting me into their restaurant but, most importantly, for welcoming me into their wonderful family.

The need to write this book grew from an inability to adequately answer questions my students asked when I critiqued their plated presentations. So, I want to thank my students for their attention and respect, and also for pushing me to grow in my professional understanding.

I would also like to thank Christian Devos, former dean of the culinary school at which I taught, for providing a working environment that inspired me, and all those who worked under him, to become a better professional as well as a better person.

There have also been many members of my professional family without whom I would not be the cook I am today. I owe particular thanks to restaurateur Allen Strong for giving me my start in a "real" restaurant; also, Mr. Jovan Trboyevic for giving me the opportunity to work in a fine-dining kitchen at a time when women were not so welcome in such establishments. Many chefs have been fundamental in my culinary progress, but I must name three who have been my paragons since I first met them in the kitchen: Chef Roland Henin, Chef Thierry Tritsch, and Chef Jean-Paul Tritsch.

Many friends, who are also professional colleagues, were very tolerant in listening to my ideas and providing feedback. Their affection helped me sustain belief in the value of my thoughts. Thanks to all of you, and in particular: Chef Lisa Gershenson, Chef Frank Chlumsky, Chef John Draz, Dr. Judy Beto, Mr. Steve Grand Pre, Chef Peggy Ryan, and Chef Heidi Hedeker.

Additionally, I would like to thank Chef Jean Joho, owner of Chicago's exquisite restaurant the Everest, for graciously lending me platters and plates used in some of the photography.

Thank you, Paul Strabbing, the book's photographer, for understanding my fear of images. I was very leery about hiring a professional who would bring his vision to my work; thank you for letting my food speak while still being shown in the best light. Your enormous kindness and talent made a very difficult segment of this project so much easier.

Thanks to Chef Christopher Koetke for introducing me to Mary Cassells at Wiley; and thanks to Wiley editors Mary Cassells and Julie Kerr for their belief in and work on this project. Thanks also to Teresa Christie, Anna Melhorn, and Jenni Lee for all their hard work and support while transforming my manuscript into a book.

I also want to thank Chef Grant Achatz for allowing me to use a menu from his restaurant, Alinea, in this book, as well as for the dining experiences I have had from his kitchens, which changed the way I looked at food.

The opportunity to research at the Lilly Library at Indiana University, Bloomington, was immensely helpful. Thanks to the Lilly staff—in particular, Mr. Joel Silver and Mr. David Frasier—for facilitating my research and granting the permission to include images from your library's culinary collection.

Thank you to all of the reviewers of the book: George Allen Akmon of Sullivan University; Nick Thompson of Aramark Higher Education; Hope Walburn of the Art Institute of Minneapolis; Mark Ainsworth of the Culinary Institute of America; and Richard Farmer, Shawn Mitchell, and Spencer McMillin of L'École Culinaire.

Finally, thanks to the readers in advance for their consideration.

—Elaine Sikorski

PROLOGUE

This book is a visual literacy primer for Culinary Arts. Its aim is to help you to be able to see, and also to create, meanings in your plate presentations.

The look a chef gives to a dish affects the flavor of the food. It does this in two ways:

1. Culinary processes actually change flavor as foods are heated, cut, or processed.

2. The mind then constructs flavors, based, in part, on the dish's appearance.

A dish also speaks to us culturally. The presentation of any dish is processed through mental associations learned throughout a person's life. As a professional cook, and then later as a chef, the mental associations that can be "read" on a plate are multidimensional.

Before you begin reading and working with this book, a record of where you are currently, in terms of plate presentations, is necessary. It will later serve as a benchmark for any changes you might make to your style as you expand your professional perspective. So before you begin Chapter 1, please do the following exercise. You will not need to look at this work again before you have finished with Chapter 7, but if you do it later, it will not provide as much insight. In the exercises at the end of Chapter 7, you will re-examine these plating diagrams.

Prologue Exercise

Choose either plate shape below. Create a plate of food by drawing in all the components you would serve, including sauce and any garnishes.

Your Field of Vision

◎ SEEING IS BELIEVING

"Do you see what I mean?" That commonplace phrase summarizes the content of this book. What you see is dependent on what you know, what you understand, and what you have been trained to see and categorize as a certain thing or relationship. Perception is a type of practice. A radiologist provides a good example of this. By examining X-ray images, radiologists can interpret the possible underlying causes of diseases. The same images, to an untrained eye, might appear perfectly normal or even unintelligible. Being able to recognize and interpret these medical images gives the radiologist a special kind of sight, and, thus, understanding of how the human body works. This, then, influences how a radiologist sees all bodies and helps define what kind of person/self a professional radiologist is. *Perception* is a type of practice that underlies how the professional self sees the world and its place in it (Daston and Galison 2007).

Although no one sees only within professional boundaries, our professional selves form strong parameters of sight. For example, a nutritionist looking at a plate of food might see calories and percentages of nutrients as fuel for the body. A food scientist might see texture as a result of chemical bonding or dispersal systems. A food service manager might see food as money, where each element on a plate represents a percentage of cost. A manufacturing executive might see food as a product that needs to fit technologies and packing design.

These different ways of seeing food lead to different ways of working with food. The nutritionist, while doing some of the same work a chef might do, is seeing, embedded in her tasks, building blocks of invisible nutrients, which changes her relationship with the food.

Which of these bowls do you see as containing food? The first bowl, on the left, is filled with edible insects. Although not all insects are safe as food, many cultures outside of the United States regularly eat insects as part of their diet. The bowl in the middle contains cherry tomatoes. During the sixteenth century, tomatoes from South America were introduced to Europe and then spread to the colonies in North America. They were originally considered poisonous. The bowl on the right contains manufactured vitamins. Food has always been a source of growth and health, but it was not until the early 1900s that supplement tablets were manufactured, allowing consumption of nutrients separate from their natural sources.

By contrast, a food scientist is applying a scientific methodology to investigate food. This is a very different relationship with food than that which chefs commonly use in their daily work. Food scientists sometimes work with chefs to relate their empirical data to practical applications in the field of research and design. Chefs working in research and design are, as the name suggest, food designers. Almost all educational disciplines have the potential to address some food component. Courses ranging from ethics to chemistry, anthropology to art, business to technology invite ways of looking at food. The way someone considers food and the purpose of that consideration are defining characteristics of a professional self; these perceptions form the relationships different types of professionals have with food.

When you look at a plate of food, what do you see? Our food considerations are learned from the earliest stages of life. They are shaped by family traditions, dining out, books, magazines, and television. Media certainly have a great effect on the look, and the looking at, of food. Food styling for commercials, magazine advertisements, and cookbook photos creates and reinforces a look of food. Individual cuisines can be identified by the appearance of certain dishes. Our expectations of a dining experience are triggered by images as diverse as a preportioned frozen dinner or a paper-wrapped hamburger to a plate with an artfully arranged meal. All these food representations are filtered through preconceptions to reinforce and influence our understanding of what is food.

Consequently, the reaction you have to what food looks like results from patterns of understanding. These patterns of understanding are the foundations for theories about food and food preparation. When we present food, we are working with an often-unarticulated theory about what food *ought* to be like. Even home cooking, which is prepared more to nourish than impress, contains a theory. It contains unconscious decisions about methods of preparation, appropriate focus foods, and look, based on the pattern of understanding we have internalized. Chefs working in "fine" dining are more conscious of these decisions, yet the articulation of culinary theory is generally not expressed as a cohesive working model. In this book, we will explore these unarticulated theories embedded in presentations. Theory allows for mental preparation prior to achieving mastery of manual skills, and theory provides greater choice and depth in your presentations once your hands catch up with your head.

◎ AN EDUCATED VIEWPOINT

As a student of culinary art, you are doing more than learning to cook; you are learning to perceive and present food in a certain way. Food presentations contain a culinary axiology: What we value, the ethics and aesthetics of culinary, are expressed in our food choices, culinary processes, and plate designs. To be able to perceive those values on a plate requires a certain way of seeing: a chef's sight.

The professional chef's way of looking translates foods' visual forms into mind flavors. In looking, chefs anticipate what the food will taste like. Chefs also understand that certain food choices, methods of preparation, and forms of food signal different meanings. Thus, a chef sees *taste* in both senses of the word. A chef looking at a plate of food imagines flavors and how they might be perceived in the mouth, but she is also seeing *taste* as a social construct within a location and time period. Imagine a grilled pork chop. Simply by thinking about those words, your mind starts to prepare your mouth for the anticipated flavor and texture of pork. However, if you have religious or ethical objections to eating meat, or specifically, pork, then you are thinking about cultural standards: taste as a social construct that has and will change based on circumstances.

In this way, a cuisine is a cultural concept; it is a system that has developed and been formalized over a length of time into a way of sequencing meals, pairing flavors, utilizing certain technologies, and assigning different values to foods. Hearth-based food systems, developed from home cooking, are types of cultural cuisines, which is why these kinds of food systems are referred to as ethnic cuisines. An ethnic cuisine may also be stratified to different economic classes or differentiated into categories of more formal celebratory meals and everyday foods.

The work done by paid cooks in restaurants, hotels, catering venues, institutions, and homes while participating in these cuisines, defined in part by geography and politics, is also part of a *Professional cuisine*. Professional cuisine has developed much like national or regional cuisines, but it reaches beyond land and political borders; its way of sequencing meals, assigning values to foods, pairing flavors, and using technologies is advanced through culinary education.

Professional cuisine developed much more slowly before the advent of readily available printed materials; it was

CUISINE AS A CULTURAL SYSTEM

Cuisine = Cultural System
Assigned Food Values
Flavor Associations
Types of Meals
Technologies Used

Hearth-based
Professional Cuisine
Home Cooking
Ethnic Cuisines/Regional Cuisines
Economic Considerations/Social Class
Everyday Nourishment
Purpose of Eating
Celebratory

passed through the generations from master cook to apprentice. It was more easily spread with the creation of trade schools and accessible printed material, which helped strengthen Professional cuisine as a distinct body of knowledge. The ability to easily publish and distribute cookbooks, view television cooking shows, post information on the Internet, and attend an academic culinary school has allowed Professional cuisine to rapidly reach millions of cooks around the globe.

Professional cuisine is perceived and created by chefs using these parameters:

◆ Associate flavors

◆ Utilize cooking processes

◆ Assign values to foods

◆ Sequence meals

The way food is presented on a plate, now often referred to as *plating,* is a chef's visual communication of these parameters. Plated food is made up of forms and patterns that are a type of visual language. The way a chef chooses to plate is, in part, a personal expression of creativity but also represents participation in the visual language of Professional cuisine. To be able to plate well requires culinary visual literacy. Just as knowledge of the alphabet and grammar are basic components of written literacy, literacy also ultimately requires an understanding of concepts shared by the culture of the language. Similarly, acquiring the visual literacy of Professional cuisine relies on an understanding of its materials, methods, and techniques, in combination with an awareness of a culinary culture.

When you enter a culinary art program, you already have a cultural background of food. You have been eating and looking at food for most of your life. The primary goal of any culinary art program is to enable you to prepare food—to cook it well and safely. But there is a difference between the older concept of cooking school and the newer idea of a culinary art program. Cooking is the foundation of culinary art. Cooking is our craft. It involves all the skills and technical knowledge necessary to prepare food for consumption. If the prepared food is to be sold, it involves the trade, or the business of hospitality. Culinary art rests entirely on these foundations, craft and trade, but it implies something more. It implies a binding of the two foundational knowledge sets with an aesthetic element.

(Craft + Trade) Aesthetic = Culinary Art

◎ AESTHETICS: ART VERSUS CRAFT

Throughout most of history, the artist and the artisan (craftsperson) were one and the same. The notion of what is beautiful was very much invested in what was also useful. The word *art* simply implied a skilled application of knowledge. During the seventeenth century, however, the meaning of the word *art* became more associated with creativity and less associated with technical skill. During the eighteenth and nineteenth centuries, for an object to be considered art, it had to be nonfunctional as well as beautiful. Thus, a vase with decoration applied to it was not an art object even if it was beautiful, because it served a purpose (OED, art, 2011).

The word *aesthetic* has an extensive background and needs to be defined for its use within a culinary context. Originally, the word was derived from Greek, where it signified sensuous perception. During the eighteenth century, the word *aesthetic* came to define a field of philosophical inquiry. At the core of this inquiry, fundamental questions centered on creating divisions between objects and people's experience in relation to them. *Aesthetic* objects were those that did not have a practical function. Aesthetic experiences happened in relation to these types of objects and could not include considerations about how to use such objects for business endeavors or personal profit (OED, aesthetic, 2011). During this same time period in Western Europe, scholars were debating the categories of human knowledge, laying the foundations for many of the disciplines now found in universities. In articulating these different fields of study, aesthetic criteria were used to separate the fine arts from the applied arts. On this basis, the fine arts developed as being more important in intellectual scope than the practical applied arts. These Western European cultural concepts eventually spread to the United States.

The *fine arts* were originally divided into five categories: painting, sculpture, music, poetry, and architecture. In contrast, the *applied arts*—what is sometimes also referred to as *craft*—were based in utility and trade. These arts included such things as textiles, woodworking, glass blowing, and ceramics (Shiner 2001).

These concepts were used to distinguish the fine arts:

◆ Symbolic

◆ Unique

◆ Contemplative

◆ Communicative

◆ Nonfunctional

◆ Genius

◆ Imagination

These characteristics were used to define the field of applied arts:

◆ Practical

◆ Repeatable

◆ Decorative

◆ Rule-based

◆ Commercial

- ◆ Mechanical
- ◆ Traditional
- ◆ Useful

The philosophical division between applied arts and the more valued fine arts was a distinction between pleasures of the body or of the mind, between useful or nonfunctional objects of beauty. As a result, the field of aesthetics became a discourse centering on the fine arts and nonfunctional beauty. The concept of good *Taste* or aesthetics evolved through many meanings; at turns it was considered rational judgments about what is beautiful, to intuitive judgments based on an "internal sense" of what is beautiful.

These thought developments affected not only art but also the general culture of different periods, and, correspondingly, perceptions of food and cooking. Cooks have struggled with this deflation for a long time. It is a large part of why the term culinary art is used instead of the simpler craft designation, cooking. The title of culinary art allows for the acknowledgment that Professional cuisine contains aesthetic substance as an integral component—which is an enhancement to the prerequisite craft of cooking.

During the twentieth century, the idea that Art had to be beautiful changed. Notice that the word *art* was capitalized in the last sentence. As the word evolved, Art with a capital "A" came to represent the concepts of fine art. *Art* began to take on some of the meanings of an older word: artifice. If the word *artifice* is used at all today, it generally is used to imply some sort of trickery, but originally the most dominant meaning of artifice was that of something person-made in contrast to being natural or existing in nature. So twentieth-century Art might not possess technical virtuosity or beauty, but was person-made in an effort to communicate. Using these standards:

- ◆ Art is a separation from the natural world.
- ◆ Craft, on the other hand, is embodied in nature. It extrapolates solutions from nature to help solve the needs of the body.
- ◆ Craft traditions have two fundamental criteria: the materials shape the direction of the work and the results serve a purpose (Risatti 2007).

During the late twentieth century and into the twenty-first century, the differences between art and craft became less rigid. Museums now often contain not only fine art pieces but items

The Art of Carving Oranges. Oranges are ready to eat foods and can also be used as ingredients in dishes. This engraving provides examples of adding aesthetic value by carving oranges tableside before serving them to the diner. From L'art de trancher la viande, & toutes sortes de fruits, nouvellement à la françoise, by Pierre Petit, escuyer tranchant (Lyon: ca 1647).

Courtesy Lilly Library, Indiana University, Bloomington, Indiana.

that were traditionally considered to be craft objects. Thus, the idea of *aesthetics* as a value divorced from the pragmatic world has again evolved into a more inclusive definition, recognizing the value of connection to the communal experience of all types of objects.

◎ ARTISTIC COOKERY

An artist creates Art. An artisan makes craft objects. And, just as Art was separated out of the artisan's workshop, the process of craft development was to be isolated and designated as a separate field: design. Design is part of the craft process. Through exposure to and work with different materials and forms, artisans form a relationship with their materials and the forms they can express. After mastering the basic techniques and possibilities of the materials, artisans often improve standard objects or develop a new style. As industry and technology developed, this design process embedded in craft work became a specialized field. Designers today create plans, drawings, and/or prototypes of objects that will be manufactured by other people. Design exhibits once displayed only in specialized design museums are now also being showcased in previously traditional fine arts–only museums.

The museum might seem far from the kitchen, but these changes affect the culinary culture. What is exhibited in traditionally "fine" art museums are examples of these boundary shifts in categorizing and understanding human creativity. The concepts of art, craft, and design, and how aesthetics relate to these fields, are evolving. Culinary art has, at turns, been considered too domestic, too commercial or, interestingly enough, too ephemeral to be a worthy subject of art, craft, or design studies. However, this, too, is changing. In 2006, Spanish Chef Ferran Adrià, of elBulli Restaurant, was the first chef to ever be presented with the Raymond Loewy Lucky Strike Designer Award. This award, presented since 1991, is given to honor designers whose work "has helped improve the social and cultural conditions of everyday life" (Lucky Strike Design Award 2006). Then in 2007, Chef Adrià was the first chef ever to be invited to participate in DOCUMENTA. This world-renowned contemporary art exhibition has taken place every five years in Kassel, Germany since 1955. (Bibliothekskatalog 2011; DOCUMENTA 2011).

FIGURE 1.3

"This is not food." Inspired by the René Magritte painting titled *The Treason of Images*, which is an image of a pipe with the disclaimer that this is not a pipe, this plate of food is not real food. It cannot be eaten, so it should be thought about differently than real food presentations. To add to the complexity, this image is of a plate holding a piece of edible printed paper, which could be eaten if, in fact, it was set before you and not just an image on a page.

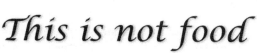

This is not food

Aesthetics, historically, was the study of sensuous perception as it relates to non-functional objects centered on "the Philosophy of Taste, the theory of Fine Arts, (and) the science of the Beautiful" (Hamilton 2011). Today, the word is more generally used to describe the sensuous properties of all types of things. Aesthetic considerations are about the look and feel of the surface of things.

However, underlying the surface is the functional. We may be attracted to eyeglasses because of shape or color, but more important is how well we can see when we put them on. The corrective lenses are the functional substance of the glasses. There is a tension between the substance and the surface. The tension is in balancing performance and functionality with look and feel (Postrel 2003).

This is also true when we plate food. We are trying to balance the functional properties of cooking and flavor with the look and mouth-feel of our presentation. The texture we give to certain foods creates a different mouth-feel, a different sensual perception of the food. Texture is often the intersection between flavor and appearance. This tension, or sometimes trade-off, between the look and the flavor of food is the central question in food presentations.

This tension between surface and substance is important in many fields of design. "Form follows function" is an often-heard phrase, meaning that the look of something should be determined by its purpose (Sullivan 1896). "Form follows emotion" is a more recent phrase coined by Industrial Designer Hartmut Esslinger (Van Hout 2006). The phrase suggests that beyond functionality, the aesthetics of something should resonate with the users' feelings and beliefs.

Culinary art, once the craft of cooking has been mastered, is a design process. The look given to food might express a modernist belief that "form follows function" or a more "postmodern" idea that "form follows emotion," as seen in the *Techno-emotive* style of Professional cuisine, presented in chapter 8. Techno-emotive cooking relies on scientific understandings of molecular gastronomy to create food that endeavors to provoke an emotional response from diners. As an example, a presentation of foam that tastes like guacamole brings an emotional element into the dish. Looking at such a green foam does not cause the brain to automatically think of avocadoes; thus, when tasted, the diner is engaged and delighted.

A Quick Glance

A plate of food expresses a worldview. Your viewpoint is developed from a personal background and then educated to join in the tradition of Professional cuisine. Culinary art reunites scholarly divisions of craft, design, and art into a holistic practice. Our practice is first about supplying safe nourishment and then pleasure. The aesthetic multiplier represents all the ways that chefs have developed to create pleasure that goes beyond sustenance.

In the following chapter, I will suggest a way of organizing your research in culinary design based on menus. Chapters 3 to 7 explore styles within Professional cuisine and extrapolate design theories inherent in these styles. Chapter 8 considers the possibility of a new style emerging in Professional cuisine. In chapters 9 to 11, the craft of cooking is related to design methods. Chapter 12 addresses how to critique presentations. Finally, chapter 13 explores what our choices express.

Some final reminders before beginning:

◆ Designing food is the work of a chef. First, you must be a great cook.

◆ Images affect professional beliefs and how practitioners make new images. (As photographic technology improved and became more accessible, artistic painting became less about realistic images.) Try to look at as much real food as possible.

◆ Pictures of food are not food. They are (re)presentations of presentations. Do not become seduced by photographers' and stylists' art. Think about what is best for the eating experience.

◆ There are many diverse food cultures that a chef uses in Professional cuisine. Become very familiar with at least one tradition before you branch out.

◆ We, in the Profession, are in a very fortunate position. Many of the world's people have inadequate supplies of food and clean water.

QUERIES & INQUIRIES

1. Define the word *food* without doing any research. Think about the question, "Is everything that is edible food?" If you answer no, what makes some edible things food while other edible substances are not food?

2. Why is it important to define Professional cuisine?

3. When food is organized into a system, is it always considered a cuisine? Consider the definition of cuisine provided in this chapter; are there other ways to define food systems? Does it make sense to think about fast-food cuisine? What are or might these systems be called?

4. What do you think are aesthetic considerations? What type of objects do they apply to?

5. What is the difference between art, craft, and design? Find an image or object related to food that represents each of these areas.

6. Is food-styling a type of Art, cooking, or design? How do food-styled images affect the perception of food?

7. Can ingredients ever be prepared to be both Art and food?

CITATION AND REFERENCE MATERIALS

Bibliothekskatalog. documenta Archiv for the Art of the 20th and 21st Centuries. © documenta Archiv © 2008 Ex Libris (Deutschland) GmbH. Retrieved April 1, 2011. alephino.documentaarchiv.de/alipac/-/sysix?SCAN_CODE=ALL%3AART&SCAN_START=documenta+12.

Daston, Lorraine, and Peter Galison. *Objectivity*. New York: Zone Books, 2007.

DOCUMENTA. documenta Archiv for the Art of the 20th and 21st Centuries. n.d. Retrieved April 1, 2011. www.kassel.de/miniwebs/documentaarchiv_e/08194/index.html>.

Hamilton, William S. *Lecture on Metaphysics* (1859) in OED section "illustrate history of word" "aesthetic, adj. and n." OED Online. March 2011. Oxford University Press. Retrieved April 1, 2011. www.oed.com/view/Entry/3237?redirectedFrom=aesthetic.

Lucky Strike Designer Award. 2006 Raymond Loewy Foundation. www.raymondloewyfoundation.com/en/lucky-strike-designer-award.html.

Mennell, Stephen. *All Manners of Food*. 2nd ed. Chicago: University of Illinois Press, 1996, pp. 64–69.

OED Online. "aesthetic, adj. and n." March 2011. Oxford University Press. Retrieved April 1, 2011. www.oed.com/view/Entry/3237?redirectedFrom=aesthetic.

OED Online. "art, n.1." March 2011. Oxford University Press. Retrieved April 1, 2011. www.oed.com/view/Entry/11125?rskey=vMilx4&result=1.

Risatti, Howard. *A Theory of Craft*. Chapel Hill: The University of North Carolina Press, 2007.

Postrel, Virginia. *The Substance of Style*. New York: HarperCollins publishers, 2003.

Shiner, Larry. *The Invention of Art*. Chicago: University of Chicago Press, 2001.

Sullivan, Louis H. "The Tall Office Building Artistically Considered." *Lippincott's Monthly Magazine* (March 1896): 403–409. Retrieved April 1, 2011. Book contributor: Research Library, The Getty Research Institute. www.archive.org/details/tallofficebuildi00sull.

Van Hout, Marco. "Getting Emotional With. . . . Hartmut Esslinger." *Design & Emotion: The emotional experience of products, services and brands*. (August 15, 2006). Retrieved April 1, 2011. www.design-emotion.com/2006/08/15/getting-emotional-with-hartmut-esslinger/.

Images

Petit, Pierre. *L'art de trancher la viande, & toutes sortes de fruits, nouvellement à la françoise, par Pierre Petit, escuyer tranchant*. Lyon: ca 1647. Manuscript. Courtesy Lilly Library, Indiana University, Bloomington, Indiana.

2

The Plate in Context

◎ REPERTOIRE

In *Professional cuisine,* plating well requires a considerable amount of prior cooking knowledge; otherwise, food is arranged more like a food stylist would approach a plate. This chapter outlines a system for organizing the necessary prerequisite culinary knowledge in order to see plates like a chef. This type of sight, remember, involves more than the surface appearance; it requires a working knowledge of food's functional context.

The functional context of food is observable to a cook working in a professional kitchen. It fits within a menu designed for a particular meal or meals. The menu is generally developed around a unifying influence of ingredients and cooking methods from a national or regional cuisine.

Professional cuisine, unlike regional or national cuisines, changes more rapidly, is more inclusive, and does not rely on any one set of ingredients. It gathers techniques, methods, ingredients, and meal and menu patterns from many sources and translates them for a commercial kitchen. Globalization and digital culture have created an information overload of available foods and cooking systems. Because of this, successful plate presentation requires a viewpoint, a focus of understanding, a guiding context.

Before cooking was taught in schools, a cook learned a repertoire, a set of *dishes* that could be executed well. Then, when the cook had mastered a repertoire of dishes, the cooking methods and techniques embedded in them could be applied to different ingredients to create different dishes. Often times in culinary schools, cooks are taught methods of cooking, which are abstractions taken from experience of a wide range of dishes. Think about how we learn to cook at home. Generally, we learn a dish and do it on many occasions, later making adjustments to suit the ingredients at hand or the preferred tastes of family. When we learn from abstractions, we sometimes neglect the importance of building a repertoire. **So, the first important requirement of successful plating is: Establish a repertoire of dishes that you can execute well**.

◯ FINDING A FOCUS

Developing a repertoire creates a relationship with foods. Your hands come to intimately know properties of certain foods and how to adapt them to different dishes later. From this collection of dishes that you like and can prepare well, you are able to understand more abstract cooking concepts. It is the focus of your culinary viewpoint. From this focus, you will then need to situate these dishes in their traditional uses.

When you learn to cook in a school, the emphasis is generally on methods of cookery, not developing a repertoire. The methods of cooking that you learn were abstracted out of the vast collection of dishes from successful chefs, but underlying these methods is a viewpoint. The viewpoint in the United States is based on the organizing principles of the Classical French cuisine. The Classical French menu originally structured the workstations in commercial kitchens. It separated hot from cold, it separated roasting from sauté, it delineated mother sauces that were the basis for all other sauces, and it placed foods and flavors into hierarchies. As Professional cuisine has become more global, and as U.S. Professional cuisine has evolved, national and international concepts have been patched into this foundation. To work well in another cooking system, you need to understand the framework of that cuisine's methodology: the way chefs working with that tradition associate flavors, utilize cooking processes, assign values to foods, and sequence meals.

Once a cook has mastered enough techniques and methods by practicing her repertoire of dishes, she is ready to consider becoming a chef. A chef arranges dishes into a plated presentation to fit a menu that cooks will copy. These arrangements are what constitute a meal and menu sequence. There are, of course, foods that are prepared that are neither part of a meal nor a menu—they are snacks. **So, the second and third requirements of successful plating are: Be able to define various types of meals and snacks, and know the standard courses of menus**.

Dish or Plate?

Before continuing to explain this essential pre-plate knowledge, two terms need to be differentiated: plate and dish. These words are often used interchangeably. However, in this book, a *dish* is not a piece of serviceware. The idea of a *dish* centers on combining flavors through a cooking process. The construction of a *plate,* or today commonly referred to as plating, focuses on the look of presented *dishes*. It is a design process. Plating uses food ingredients, or *dishes,* already cooked or structured and arranges them on serviceware.

◎ SEQUENCING FOODS

Recognizing the category of food you are trying to present comes first. Breakfast, lunch, dinner, and brunch are the standard meals of the United States. Snacks can be anything eaten between them but may also include hors d'oeuvre, cocktail buffet food, and passed appetizers.

The category of food will help determine the portion size and types of food chosen to present. Then within that category, define the type of service that will be used. Service style is dependent on price point and time of expected dining experience. For example, fast food is, as the name implies, meant to be served and eaten quickly at a minimum price. **So, the fourth requirement of successful plating is: Define the Culinary Context, which consists of Food Category, Price Point, and Service Style, before designing a plate**.

The Culinary Context

Consider a lunch menu: Lunch portions might be smaller than dishes offered at dinner time, or the accompanying dinner side dishes might be absent. The food choices might also differ between lunch and dinner; instead of a porterhouse steak, a sandwich steak might be offered. Also affecting the food choices at lunch are the factors of price and time. Thus, lunch service might be a counter-ordered meal delivered to the table rather than a dinner meal with full table service.

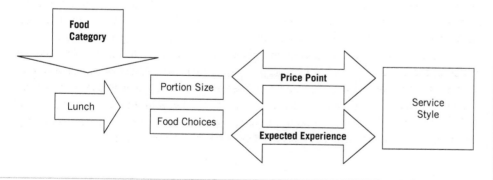

Any one of these parameters can be the first, but they all must be considered before creating the look of the food. After these parameters are set, delineate the menu sequence used within the service style. Is the customer expected to eat one dish or multiple courses during this food experience? If it is a multiple course experience, what is the order of the foods or the courses of the menu? Continuing the lunch versus dinner example, the lunch customer might be expected to eat only one central plate, which presents dishes such as a steak sandwich with fries, while the dinner customer might be more likely to order soup, followed by a steak dish, and finish with a dessert. Thus, the menu sequence for lunch is simply the main course, while for dinner the menu sequence is appetizer, then main course, followed by dessert.

The order in which certain dishes are served customarily has a regional or national cultural orientation and always has historical roots. Generally, formal meals served on important occasions or to important people have the greatest number of courses. Abbreviated sequences are extrapolated out of formal meals to form more casual menus. For example, the menu for a formal wedding meal in the United States might have the following courses:

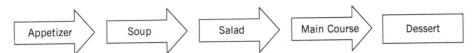

A cook that understands how formal meals are structured can then create more casual styles of meals by using only some of the courses of the formal meal, such as the abbreviated sequence for an informal wedding meal: appetizer, main course, dessert. Similarly, knowing the courses of formal meals from different regional or national cuisines allows the cook to create sensible categories of offerings on an à la carte menu.

Essential to Professional cuisine is the principle that plating is dependent on menu structure and service style. The structure of the menu categories and their subsequent dishes, in creating flavor affinities and flavor ordering, help to construct the guidelines for plating. Frequently, foods are chosen and presented based on color, shape, height, or texture; this often leads to presentations that are superficial and to eating experiences that are commonplace. However, in Professional cuisine, plating is a meaningful design process. The menu is the working document of a chef; it is our primary research source. Ingredients, purpose, and tradition are acknowledged in a menu. **So, the fifth requirement of successful plating is: Research menus to provide the framework of culinary knowledge.**

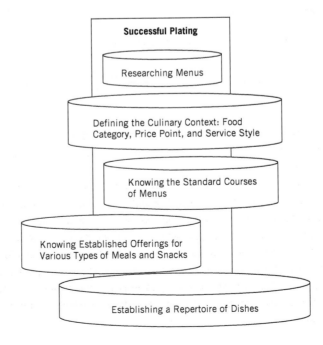

◎ MENU RESEARCH

To begin your menu research, you need a collection of menus. Base your collection on food category, price point, and style of service. Here is an example:

Food Category:	Dinner
Price Point:	Expensive
Service Style:	Table, Plated
Menu Format:	Special Event

These parameters set the Culinary Context. The following chart suggests other possibilities for such parameters.

Food Category	Price Point	Service Style	Menu Format
Breakfast	Low	Table	À la Carte
Lunch	Moderate	• Family Style / Platter	Special Event
Small Bites	Expensive	• Plated	• Tasting Menu
Dinner		• Table Side / Platter	• Daily Special (Blue Plate, Plat du Jour)
Brunch		Banquet	
Snack		Buffet	Prix Fixe (Table d'hôte)
• Passed Appetizers		Bar	Cycle
• Hors d'oeuvre		Cafeteria	
• Out of Hand		Counter and Carry	
		Take-out	
		Packaged	

Notice in the example above the table that another parameter has been added to the fourth requirement of successful plating: Menu Format. The format of a menu is a synergy of food category and service style. The format shapes what decisions the customer can make in food choices. For example, a special event menu is used once versus an à la carte menu, which is used in a restaurant for many services. A special event menu is similar to a chef's tasting menu in that the diner has few or no choices. The menu format is the kitchen's articulation of the dining experience; it frames the way food is presented to a customer. Ultimately, restaurants can be categorized by the ratio of focus foods and cooking processes offered on their menus. Generally, in à la carte menus, the more expensive the dining experience, the greater variety of cooking methods and focus foods offered. Starting in Chapter 3, the concept of a menu as a type of frame for plate presentations will be further developed.

Embedded in a plate presentation are all these understandings of where the plate fits. When chefs evaluate a plate, they intuitively see all these parameters. That is why sometimes a chef will say, "It doesn't work," or, "It's not right," because it doesn't fit in the parameters that the chef has in mind. There are, of course, many other reasons a plate may not be successful, but those considerations come later in the evaluative process.

◎ READING A MENU

When you read a menu, it is normal to first see the focus food being offered, because that is generally how we decide what to order. However, when you read a menu for research purposes, it is more advantageous to first see the cooking process applied to the focus food.

After noting the cooking process, identify focus food followed by its sauce. Next, determine what you perceive to be the dominant flavor, which can sometimes be difficult to name. You will need to create a list of flavor descriptors that are meaningful to you. What you are trying to decipher is the level of intensity of the flavor as well as the type of flavor. Finally, you need to establish the satiety value of the menu item. This is usually related to the amount of fat or carbohydrate in a dish. You might use descriptors such as heavy, rich, light, or neutral.

So, each menu item is analyzed using this flow diagram:

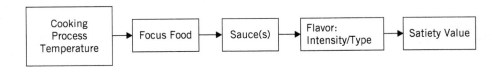

This sort of diagramming allows you see the relationship of the plate to the ones before and after it. If the customer is expected to eat multiple courses, then placing a dish with a strong flavor or high satiety flavor in the beginning of the sequence might diminish the appreciation of the subsequent dishes. Designing a plate presentation without the content of a menu-frame removes the substance of the eating experience. Even if the plate is to be a stand-alone meal, it is situated within a context of food category, price point, and service style, which theoretically suggests a type of menu. The way menus are written today has evolved from traditions established long ago, which will be explored beginning in Chapter 3.

Chefs at the White House represent the best in our profession. Researching how menus have changed at the White House reflects not only changes in Professional cuisine but also changes in national restaurant culture. Following are two White House dinner menus (Stanford L. Fox Collection). The first menu was served in 1960 during the presidency of Dwight D. Eisenhower. The second menu was served in 1993 during the presidency of Bill Clinton. I am using them to demonstrate how a menu is diagrammed, but they are also representative of different styles of formal dining. Notice how fewer courses were served in 1993; also notice the change in the language used to describe the courses. Finally, look at the sequence of cooking processes, temperatures, focus foods, sauces, and satiety value patterns in each menu. Look at how these patterns differ.

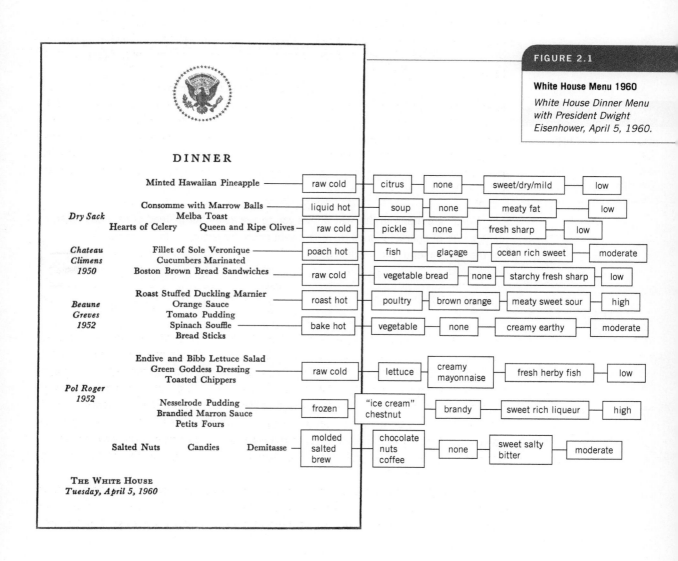

FIGURE 2.1

White House Menu 1960
White House Dinner Menu with President Dwight Eisenhower, April 5, 1960.

DINNER

Course	Process	Focus	Sauce	Flavor	Satiety
Minted Hawaiian Pineapple	raw cold	citrus	none	sweet/dry/mild	low
Consomme with Marrow Balls / Melba Toast	liquid hot	soup	none	meaty fat	low
Hearts of Celery Queen and Ripe Olives	raw cold	pickle	none	fresh sharp	low
Fillet of Sole Veronique / Cucumbers Marinated	poach hot	fish	glaçage	ocean rich sweet	moderate
Boston Brown Bread Sandwiches	raw cold	vegetable bread	none	starchy fresh sharp	low
Roast Stuffed Duckling Marnier / Orange Sauce / Tomato Pudding	roast hot	poultry	brown orange	meaty sweet sour	high
Spinach Souffle / Bread Sticks	bake hot	vegetable	none	creamy earthy	moderate
Endive and Bibb Lettuce Salad / Green Goddess Dressing / Toasted Chippers	raw cold	lettuce	creamy mayonnaise	fresh herby fish	low
Nesselrode Pudding / Brandied Marron Sauce / Petits Fours	frozen	"ice cream" chestnut	brandy	sweet rich liqueur	high
Salted Nuts Candies Demitasse	molded salted brew	chocolate nuts coffee	none	sweet salty bitter	moderate

Wines:
Dry Sack
Chateau Climens 1950
Beaune Greves 1952
Pol Roger 1952

The White House
Tuesday, April 5, 1960

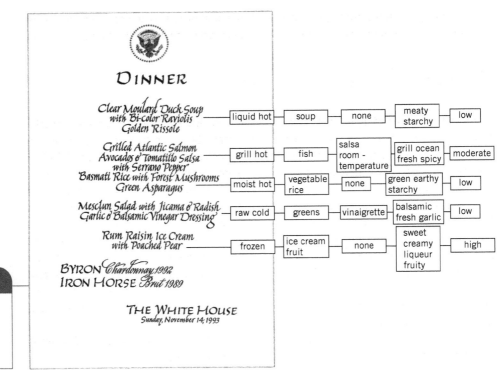

FIGURE 2.2

White House Menu 1993

White House Dinner Menu with President Bill Clinton, November 14, 1993.

Reading a menu in this way allows you to see as a chef instead of as a customer. In each group of characteristics there is a sequence; for example, in the temperature group for the 1960 menu, the sequence is:

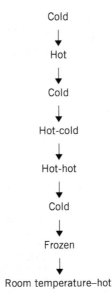

In looking at each grouping as a sequence, the chef is able to decide if the flavors are expressed well, and most importantly, if the changes from one course to the next eat well.

CREATIVITY AND TRADITION

The traditional uses of ingredients to form meals, snacks, and menu structures underlie contemporary choices. It is not a question of "creativity versus tradition, but creativity informed by tradition and tradition transformed by creativity" (Weiss 2002, pp. 98–99). For example, the newest style of professional cooking, Techno-emotive cuisine, started by deconstructing traditional flavor affinities, and then advanced to culinary constructionism (abstract cooking). A chef working at this level depends on much automatic understanding of traditional techniques and historical solutions.

No matter what area of food service you are interested in, a tradition exists. Choosing a focus area of food service and researching the way chefs in this area presented food exposes the established criteria of successful work. Historically, food fashions were generated from upscale dining restaurants or extrapolated out of home cooking. Today, the home cook is influenced by the professional sector and fine dining is influenced by technologies and foods that result from food product design.

The method for investigating any one of the divisions in these areas is the same. Begin by choosing a focus, as illustrated by the following diagram.

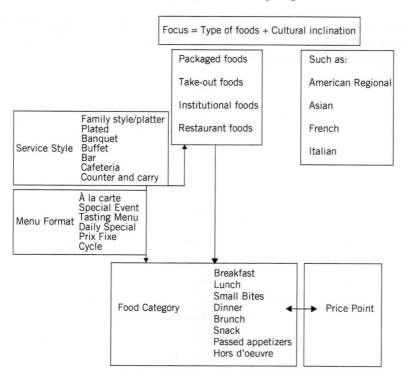

Then, find information about the earliest examples of food presentations in this area. If you are interested in research and design, you might begin by finding the first frozen meals or canned foods that were sold. If you are interested in restaurant food, you will need to narrow your research to a particular type of service experience, from fast food to fine dining. The examples of food presentations then need to be situated within the parameters of food category, price point, service style, and menu format. To illustrate, material in chapters 3 to 7 contains a research example focusing on fine dining.

Fine Dining

Fine dining isn't really the best name for this type of eating experience anymore because fine dining implies a hierarchy of taste accessible only to an elite class. Today, this type of dining experience is better called artistic or destination dining. While this type of restaurant still requires a certain economic status, the reasons people choose to dine there are less about class delineation and more about experiencing an artful perspective of considered cooking. Artistic dining is the most formalized dining experience, and as such generates the most criteria about plate presentations.

QUERIES & INQUIRIES

1. What is a culinary repertoire?

2. What is the difference between a *plate* and a *dish* as defined in this chapter?

3. What parameters set the Culinary Context?

4. What is a food category as the concept is described in this chapter? What are the food categories listed?

5. Create a list of *dishes* that you can cook well. Sort your list into food categories.

6. Look at the service styles listed and relate these styles to the types of menu formats listed. How does the format of menu relate to the type of service?

7. Collect three menus that have the same type of format for the same style of service. For example, you might choose wedding banquet menus or moderately priced lunch à la carte menus using table service. Banquet or tasting menus are the easiest to begin with, as there are not as many offering as on an à la carte menu.

a. What are the courses of the menu format you chose?

b. Following the steps on page 16 for diagramming a menu, analyze every offering on each menu and write in the processes.

c. Create charts to compare the menus by groups, such as the following for cooking process.

Group: Cooking Process	Menu 1	Menu 2	Menu 3
1st course			
2nd course			
3rd course			
4th course			
5th course			
6th course			
7th course			
8th course			
Delete or add rows to correspond to the number of courses in your menus.			

The other groupings of menu diagramming are temperature, focus food, sauce(s), flavor, and satiety value. You should prepare a chart for each group.

1. Now analyze each chart for patterns in your results. In your chosen menu format and service style, are there patterns that are always followed? For instance, do the menus always begin with a cold dish? Is sweet always at the end of the menu?

2. Explain what artistic dining is. What are other possible names for this type of dining experience?

CITATION AND REFERENCE MATERIALS

Weiss, Allen S. *Feast and Folly*. Albany: State University of New York Press, 2002, pp 98–99.

Images

White House menus purchased on eBay through the Sanford L. Fox Collection, chief of the Social Entertainments Office and director of protocol for the White House, 1960–1975.

3

Framing Culinary Art

Keep in mind that plating is always dependent on menu structure and service style. To further clarify how food presentations are affected by the service-menu association, a *culinary Art history* needs to be created. The word *Art* is capitalized because the look of food as symbols of professional beliefs is being investigated. In tracing any history, emphasis may be given to one area of concern, but affecting this area are all the technological, social, economic, and cultural concerns of any given period within that history. So, while examining food presentations of a certain period, it must be noted that these presentations also relate to many other histories of manners and customs, of kitchen technologies and personalities, and of cultural styles and fashions that are situated in time periods defined by other viewpoints.

Time periods have often been labeled by historians to signify developments in artistic styles, philosophical movements, or power structures, such as Neoclassical art during the Renaissance, or the Age of Enlightenment. Although these developments certainly affected the look of food, culinary presentations need to be framed instead by menu and service style changes, which do not fit exactly into these established periods but develop more slowly and with greater overlap. It is erroneous to think of culinary history as linear—as phases replacing the previous ones. Instead, it is more like sediments of the earth building on one another: the older layers become less and less obvious, but still shape the newer layers. It is also true that the work done by one chef influences the work of other chefs, which influences what we come to believe about what food is and should be. The mega-concept of what food is and should be, in turn, influences the work of a chef. Creating a *culinary Art history* will allow us to see taste presented not just as a means of creating flavor but also as a cultural context larger than the professional kitchen. To summarize, the way food is plated now grew from practices over a long professional tradition.

◎ culinary Art history

A period of *culinary Art history* is defined by service style and menu structure. These periods can be understood as **Frames**, which create boundaries for the presentation of foods. A change in the idea of what a meal should be changes both how menus are structured and how meals are served. This, then, is what changes a Frame in the *culinary Art history*. While considering the Frames of presentations, some cultural developments need to be noted to provide points of reference. In this history, there are three Frames, reflecting three periods, prior to the current Plate Frame, that were eventually to influence artistic dining in the United States. These early Frames are found in the dining customs and manners of the European nobility. In contrast, styles within the later frame, where the presentation boundaries are set by the plate, are more egalitarian.

◎ PRE-PLATE *culinary Art history*: THE ROOM FRAME

In the fourteenth and fifteenth centuries, the European world was not yet divided into the countries we recognize today; city-states and empires formed alliances through powerful family connections. During the Medieval and Renaissance periods, these relationships laid the foundation for a style of aristocratic dining across Western Europe. Technologically, the use of glazed ceramic serviceware and the fork were just beginning. Printed books had little influence on cooks, and images in cookbooks, such as woodcut prints, were almost absent. Gastronomically, the foods of the *New World*, such as tomatoes, potatoes, and chocolate, were just being introduced and not yet part of recipes. In art history, this period would loosely correspond to the artistic styles of International Gothic and early Renaissance.

The Frame for this period's food presentations was the *Room*. Because dining was more about the display of wealth and power of a ruling group, what any one individual ate was not important. The communal acknowledgment of social hierarchy was determined by the scale and extravagance of presented foods. For example, large platters and dishes were paraded into the chamber and placed according to the rank of the seated diners. Entire birds, predominantly peacocks and swans, were skinned with feathers on, to be rewrapped around the roasted bird before serving. The element of surprise was highly valued; pies baked empty and later filled with live birds provided such an effect. Figurative food displays, made of pastry dough or sugar called *entremets* (or sotelties), were often designed by the leading artists of the court and were the most prized food displays. These elaborate food presentations were often carried into the room between courses, which is literally what the word describes: *entre* (between) and *met* (a course); later, in the *Table Frame*, entremets would become a type of dish, and later still, in the *Platter Frame*, a type of course. Food was often molded into crowns, religious emblems, or animals. These types

"The presentation of the peacock" from the *Livre des Conquestes et faits d'Alexandre* by Jean Wauquelin, fifteenth-century French medieval manuscript.

Courtesy of "Petit Palais, Musée des Beaux-Arts de la Ville de Paris."

of illusion and figurative dishes are more mind-filling entertainment than stomach-filling nourishment, with an overall goal of abundance and distinction.

From the Room Frame, we can see concepts that are still in use today; for example, controlled surprise can be delightful, food shaped like other things is intriguing, and coloring foods can add value. The concept of making tomato roses or shaping potatoes to resemble pears is an echo from this period of food design. At this time, sweet foods were not yet separated from savory foods, a division that is blurring again today in the concept of the pre-dessert course.

Food was already seen as an important part of health. The human body was thought to have four humors; hot, moist, cold, and dry foods were prepared and combined to create equilibrium of these humors. This gave rise to some taste combinations and sequencing of foods that influenced subsequent food patterns.

PRE-PLATE *culinary Art history:* THE TABLE FRAME

As central courts and monarchies gained power during the sixteenth century, the emphasis on refinement and order in food displays grew. Geography began to take on the nation-shapes we recognize today, and more recognizable national cuisines were developing. The French distinguished themselves as the leaders in matters of style and taste. Also, cookbooks were more widespread, and table plans showing how a meal should be presented were extensive in cookbooks of the period. Serviceware became elaborate and extensive. In art history, this period would loosely correspond to the artistic styles of Rococo and Neoclassical, and the subsequent period referred to as Romanticism. Gastronomically, this was the era of *service à la française*. A course, or service, was defined by a table plan. By the early 1800s it had become formalized into three courses, three different table plans per meal—each course consisting of multiple dish categories. Thus, food presentations were now framed by the *Table*. This reflects the shift to a communal dining experience within a defined social class that orders the importance of diners and dishes.

The first table (course) was composed from dish categories of soups, hors d'oeuvre, fish, entrées, which were the large centered dishes, and relevés, which were the dishes that would replace removed dishes. For instance, a soup might have been removed after serving and a relevé of fish might have taken its place. The first course's entrées were generally associated with meats such as saddles, short loins, or tenderloins. The relevés were often fish dishes or sometimes smaller meat dishes in a sauce.

The second table (course) was composed from dish categories of roasts, cold dishes, and entremets. Entremets included hot sweet dishes and important vegetable dishes, such as asparagus with Hollandaise. The second course included slightly different kinds of meats, such as game, or possibly poultry. This course showcased the roasts.

The third table (course) was composed from dish categories of cold sweet dishes, fruits, candies, and cheeses (Dubois 1856, vii–xi, 1–16; Colquhoun, 158).

Overall, within the Table Frame, there was concern about variety of cooking methods as well as types of dishes. Italian style menus often ordered dishes by cooking method, while French style menus more often ordered by the type of meat although both traditions considered grouping dishes by temperature. This dissimilarity eventually leads to different menu sequences for these countries.

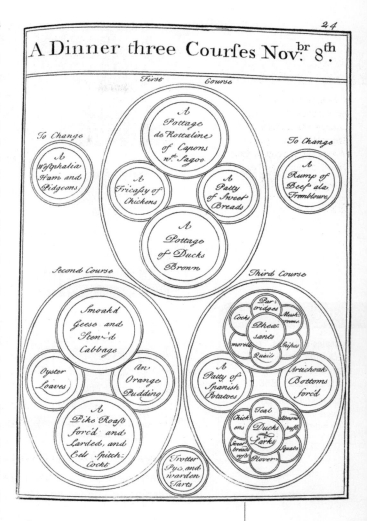

Foods were still often shaped into figurative compositions, such as castles. Examples of such presentations can be found in the color inset, Images 2, 3, and 19. Socles, bordures, and hâtelets were used to embellish dishes. These constructions of bread, noodle paste, and elaborate skewers were used for their decorative value. The height of great skewers stuck into dishes, or the building of elaborate platforms with flour-paste or bread to resemble porcelain or precious metal serviceware, gave Table food considerable separation from its natural state. In contrast to the showy spectacle presented in the Room Frame, the Table Frame highlighted sophisticated, refined, ordered presentations.

The concept of beauty changed greatly during this time period. Influenced by the concepts of the Enlightenment, rationality and mathematical order were the underpinnings of many artisans' work. Pyramids and symmetry were two visual values used to express rational beauty. The look of food displays left on the table or as part of the dessert table was greatly influenced by the look of Rococo design, with its curves and flourishes, combined with the

FIGURE 3.2

Three-course Meal: *service à la française.* A table plan for a three-course meal to be served during November shows the placement of the plates and the dishes served. From *The Complete Practical Cook* by Charles Carter, 1730.

Courtesy Lilly Library, Indiana University, Bloomington, Indiana.

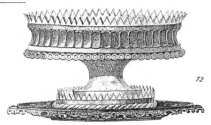

FIGURE 3.3

Examples of socles. From
La Cuisine Classique by
Chef Urbain Dubois and
Émile Bernard, 1856.

*Courtesy Lilly Library,
Indiana University,
Bloomington, Indiana.*

subject matter of Neoclassical art. An example of these influences can be seen in the geometrically designed table plan from 1758 in figure 3.5 below.

Also, scientific developments of this period increased kitchen technologies. Chefs now saw themselves as participating in the new chemical understanding by extracting essences from foods and refining their crude forms. Rarity and refinement, symmetry and order were hallmarks of this new style of cooking. Chefs working in this "modern" cuisine thought seriously about flavor. Their *nouvelle cuisine* advocated delicacy and elegance.

From this Frame comes the appreciation for geometrically shaped foods and symmetrical patterns in food presentations. Structuring height into food presentations is a design concept carried forward from this Frame. In fact, edible pedestals are still used today to create height. Examples of older, elaborate socles supporting dishes, as well as a more modern, classical use of a bread socle, are pictured in the color inset, Images 2–5, and 16. The bread base under meat in certain dishes of today, such as a crouton under Tournedos Rossini, is a vestige of this practice. Similarly, the use of skewers to create not only visual interest but also height can still be seen in the contemporary practice where semi-edible food items are stuck into the top of finished dishes, such as rosemary skewers. The modern practice of containing vegetables in potato baskets or tying green beans into little bundles is an echo from this period of food design as well.

FIGURE 3.4

**Examples of the decorative
skewers (hâtelets).** From *La
Cuisine Classique* by Chef
Urbain Dubois and Émile
Bernard, 1856.

*Courtesy Lilly Library,
Indiana University,
Bloomington, Indiana.*

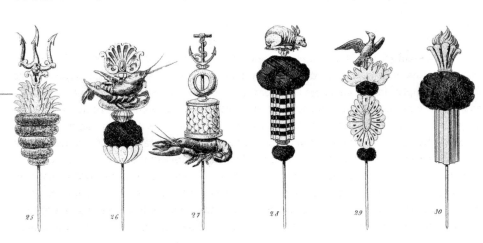

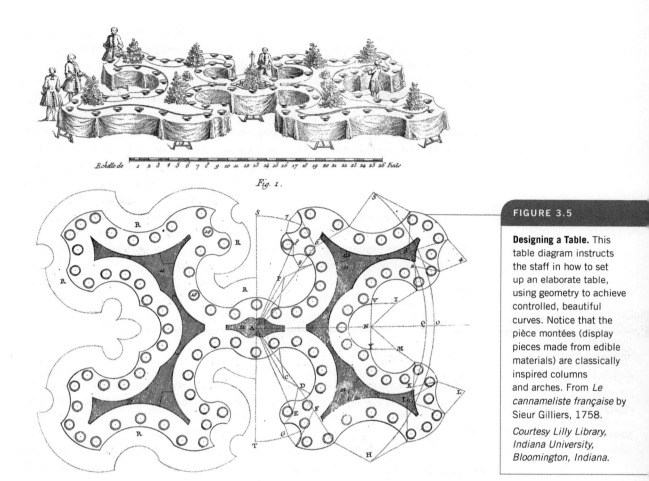

FIGURE 3.5

Designing a Table. This table diagram instructs the staff in how to set up an elaborate table, using geometry to achieve controlled, beautiful curves. Notice that the pièce montées (display pieces made from edible materials) are classically inspired columns and arches. From *Le cannameliste française* by Sieur Gilliers, 1758.

Courtesy Lilly Library, Indiana University, Bloomington, Indiana.

MOVING TOWARD THE PLATE: THE PLATTER FRAME IN *culinary Art history*

During the 1880s, the middle class was on the rise, as was urban growth; this was the era of the public sphere. The Industrial Revolution offered new economic opportunities for more people. Technologically, while black and white photography and color chromolithography were starting to be used in printed materials, many cookbooks still contained only a limited number of printed illustrations. As the Modern period of Art began, Realism replaced Romanticism, with Impressionism and Art Nouveau as examples of styles. The subject matter for Art shifted from the mythological or ideal to real people and events in their natural states. As we shall see in Chapter 4, in culinary, the Classical style very shortly begins the similar journey of presenting food in a more natural state than during the Table Frame; however, these types of artistic developments would not find parallels in food aesthetics until the Nouvelle style of plating, presented in Chapter 5, close to 100 years later.

Now, there was a whole new sector of people who could afford to dine in style. It is during this era that our modern restaurant culture began. Previously, most people dined at home. There were taverns and inns for travelers, but these types of establishments did not offer a choice in what to eat or much in the way of atmosphere. By the end of the nineteenth century, different types of restaurants had been established, with Delmonico's restaurant in New York generally credited as being the first "fine dining" establishment in the United States.

During this time of transition of power from the royal courts to a more republican culture, a newer style of service was developing, as was a transitional Frame—the Platter. *Service à la russe* began being practiced in the first half of the nineteenth century; it was a reaction to problems in the previous menu Frame of *service à la française*. Placing all the foods on the table for each course of a meal required not only a great amount of food but also resulted in the displayed food coming to room temperature. Diners were also limited in their food choices by what was within polite reach. *Service à la russe* strove to solve these problems by sequencing foods into courses that could be experienced by all diners and served at the intended temperature, framed on a Platter.

Service at the Table

Traditional

Service à la française	Originally used during the Table Frame, this type of service was like an elaborate family-style meal where all the foods are placed on the table and diners help themselves to whatever is in polite reach.
Service à la russe	Originally used during the transitional Platter Frame, this type of service required a server to present and serve guests from platters brought in a sequence to the table.

Contemporary

Service à la carte	The emphasis of restaurant style service replaces older service styles, which were based on dining in a private home. Restaurant customers order from a menu. Not all the diners at the table eat the same dishes, or even the same menu courses.
English style service	Wait-staff present platters to diners and serve them from the platters, acting in place of the table's host.
American style service	Wait-staff bring finished plates from the kitchen to each diner.

	European	American
French style service	Wait staff present platters of food to diners, who help themselves from the platters; or, platters are left on the table for diners to help themselves.	Wait staff, working from a guéridon table side, finish preparing and plating the food for each diner.
Russian style service	Wait staff, working from a guéridon table side, finish preparing and plating the food for each diner.	Wait staff present platters to diners and serve them from the platters.

By 1893, when Charles Ranhofer, chef of Delmonico's restaurant, published *The Epicurean*, there were still explanations of how to execute *service à la française*, as well as the newer style of *service à la russe*, and their dependent menu structures. A generalized course structure for a menu at this time of transition to *service à la russe* would be as follows:

Cold Hors d'oeuvre: often oysters on the half shell

Soup: possibly one clear, one thick

Hot Hors d'oeuvre: timbales, croustades, mousselines, bouchées, etc.

Fish: sometimes not listed, as the fish often functioned as a relevé, or, less often, as an entrée; with shellfish sometimes designated as a hot hors d'oeuvre

Removes (Relevés):   solid joints, saddles veal, lamb, venison, beef tenderloin or middle short ribs, turkey, capon, goose; may have been accompanied by vegetables

Entrées: starting with the heaviest to the lightest, sometimes accompanied by a vegetable; generally not a winged game but, rather, small cuts of meat or poultry often poached or braised

– – –

Punch or sorbet

– – –

Roasts: generally game, large birds, such as turkey, or, less commonly, beef

(Salad can be served with the Roast course, separately as a course, or in the next course of Cold Dishes.)

Cold Dishes: terrines of foie gras, galantines, chaud-froid; cold lobster presentations, etc.; possibly served with a salad in other than French menus, which do not allow salad with foie gras

Legumes: previously called savory entremets: these are vegetables in sauce, such as asparagus and Hollandaise

Cheese: IN FRENCH-INSPIRED MENUS

Entremets Sucrés
  Hot Sweet Dishes   puddings, fried creams, fritters, crêpes, omelets, soufflé

– – –

  Cold Sweet Dishes: jellies, bavarois, blanc-manges, large cakes

Dessert: CHEESE IN ENGLISH INSPIRED MENUS; or *savouries* (highly seasoned hors d'oeuvre), fresh fruit, bonbons, candied fruits, jams, pyramids, frozen puddings, ices, small fancy cakes

Coffee and Cordials

   (Ranhofer 1971, 2, 108) (Montagné 1977, 585–587)

51

First Course thus,

A Seventeen Dish Table.

Second Course thus.

FIGURE 3.6

Order and Symmetry of Dishes. A table plan for two courses in a meal. Each course is to consist of 17 dishes that are placed in a hierarchy radiating out from the center dishes. Note the sizes of the different dishes and the symmetry used. From *The Complete Practical Cook* by Charles Carter, 1730.

Courtesy Lilly Library, Indiana University, Bloomington, Indiana.

The lines drawn between the various courses in the menu above are mine; they correspond roughly to what would have been the dishes included in the first, second, and third courses of *service à la française* within the Table Frame, where all these dishes would have been placed on the table at once. The punch or sorbet now served in a progression of dishes as the break between what was the first table and the second table.

Notice that the possible placement of salads differs from French to British menus. This is an interesting difference because cheese in English menus would be served last with something like Port wine, while in the French menus, the cheese is served following the salad and cold dishes, which traditionally needed no wine or a white wine. The progression of flavors in this form of elaborate menu allows for an extensive discussion of how temperatures and foods are best appreciated, as well as how beverages fit the menu structure.

Throughout the Table and Platter Frames, dishes were increasingly organized into categories. The first major division was the separation of sweet dishes into their own course at the end of the service. As this was happening, other dishes were assigned central placement as being the most important, or the main dishes. Medium-sized dishes circled the central dishes, with the smallest dishes placed around the outside of the table. The word *hors d'oeuvre*, used to categorizes these dishes, literally means outside of the main work. As this hierarchy of placement developed, the ingredients and cooking methods with their attendant sauces were also being ranked by association.

Then, when these categories were used as course names in a sequenced menu, the ordering of foods, flavors, and cooking processes began to be formalized.

The most important design element of this transitional Frame was the ordering of foods into established courses on a menu. Another lasting effect was the presentation of platters from which food was moved onto a plate, in front of the diner, by service staff. A final important concept is symmetry, paramount in Table presentation, which greatly influenced platters being styled almost like miniature tables. Symmetry is still a design pattern used in some plate arrangements today.

Enduring Design Elements from the Three Historical Frames: Room, Table, and Platter

Design Element	Begins in the:
Shaping foods into figurative forms	Room Frame
Symmetry	Table Frame
Ordering foods into established courses	Table Frame, solidifies in the Platter Frame
Courses consist of one dish	Platter Frame
Food is moved by service staff to plates	Platter Frame

Platter menus and *à la russe* service were at first designed for private, at home dining prepared by professional chefs. Banquets given in, or large tables hosted at, restaurants organized their service to be similar to these at-home experiences. As fine dining became more a part of the public sphere, diners at the same table sought more individualized choices. This required a new style of menu and service, *à la carte service*, and is the beginning of the next Frame.

Service à la française and *service à la russe* were both practiced during the same time span. Restaurants also already existed during this same historical period using *à la carte* service. To better understand plating, it is important to distinguish each service style and its menu separately and each as defining a culinary Frame. Also note that even though Art is now considered to be in the Modern period, with such movements as Impressionism and Post-Impressionism happening, it would be more than 50 years before food took an Impressionistic turn. These three historical Frames—Room, Table, and Platter—are presented as the briefest of backgrounds for the subject of modern restaurant service and thus plated presentations.

QUERIES & INQUIRIES

This chapter is primarily concerned with setting the background of plating. For that reason, being able to define terms and outline the *culinary Art history* provided in this chapter are the main objectives.

1. Define the following terms and concepts: *culinary Art history*, figurative food, socle, and hâtelet.

2. Explain the following types of service: *service à la française*, *service à la russe*, *service à la carte*, English style service, American style service, French style service, and Russian style service.

3. What is plating dependent upon?

4. What defines a Frame in the *culinary Art history*?

5. What are the two *culinary Art history* Frames prior to Platter? What type of service and menu is used in each?

6. What changes cause a new Frame to be defined?

7. What is the style of service and the menu format used in the Platter frame?

8. Find a historic cookbook written by a professional chef that corresponds to each of the three Frames outlined: Room, Table, Platter.

9. What is an entremet in the Room Frame? in the Table Frame? in the Platter Frame?

CITATION AND REFERENCE MATERIALS

Attar, Dena. "Keeping Up Appearances: The Genteel Art of Dining in Middle-Class Victorian Britain." Wilson, C. Anne, ed. *The Appetite and the Eye: Visual Aspects of Food and Its Presentation within Their Historic Context*. Second Leeds Symposium on Food History and Traditions, April 1987, with additional papers. Edinburgh: Edinburgh University Press, 1991, pp. 123–140.

Boyle, Tish, and Timothy Moriarty. *Grand Finales; The Art of the Plated Dessert*. New York: John Wiley & Sons, Inc., 1997.

Boyle, Tish, and Timothy Moriarty. *A Modernist View of Plated Desserts*. New York: John Wiley & Sons, Inc., 1998.

Brears, Peter. "Decoration of the Tudor and Stuart Table." Wilson, C. Anne, ed. *The Appetite and the Eye: Visual Aspects of Food and Its Presentation within Their Historic Context*. Second Leeds Symposium on Food History and Traditions, April 1987, with additional papers. Edinburgh: Edinburgh University Press, 1991, pp. 56–97.

Colquhoun, Kate. *Taste: The Story of Britain Through Its Cooking*. New York: Bloomsbury, 2007, p. 158.

Culinary Institute of America. *Remarkable Service*. Hoboken, NJ: John Wiley & Sons, Inc., 2009, pp. 30–58.

Dubois, Urbain, and Emile Bernard. *La Cuisine Classique études pratiques, raisonnées et de l'école Française appliqué au service a la russe*. Paris: Chez Les Auteurs, 1856. University of Washington Libraries. pp. vii–xi, 1–16.

"France, 1400–1600 A.D." In *Heilbrunn Timeline of Art History*. New York: The Metropolitan Museum of Art, 2000–(October 2002). Retrieved April 4, 2011, at www.metmuseum.org/toah/ht/?period=08&ion=euwf.

"France, 1600–1800 A.D." *In Heilbrunn Timeline of Art History*. New York: The Metropolitan Museum of Art, 2000–(October 2003). Retrieved April 4, 2011, at www.metmuseum.org/toah/ht/?period=09&ion=euwf.

"France, 1800–1900 A.D." *In Heilbrunn Timeline of Art History*. New York: The Metropolitan Museum of Art, 2000–(October 2004). Retrieved April 4, 2011, at www.metmuseum.org/toah/ht/?period=10&ion=euwf.

Henderson, Mary F. *Practical Cooking and Dinner Giving*. New York: Harper & Brothers, 1877. Michigan State Universities Libraries Digital Collection: The Historic Cookbook Project: Feeding America. Retrieved February 5, 2011, digital.lib.msu.edu/projects/cookbooks/display.cfm?TitleNo=27&PageNum=1 (pp. 348–353).

Kaufman, Cathy K. "Structuring the Meal: the Revolution of service à la russe." Walker, Harlan, ed. *The Meal: Proceedings of the Oxford Symposium on Food and Cookery 2001*. Great Britain: Prospect Books, 2002, pp. 123–133.

Laudan, Rachel. "Birth of the Modern Diet." *Scientific American Reports* 16 (2) (2005): 4–11.

Mennell, Stephen. *All Manners of Food*. 2nd ed. Chicago: University of Illinois Press, 1996, pp. 47–64.

Montagné, Prosper. *The New Larousse Gastronomique*. New York: Crown, 1977; American Editor Charlotte Turgeon originally copyright Librairie Larousse, Paris, 1960, pp. 585–587.

Poulain, Jean-Pierre; Neirinck. *Histoire de la Cuisine et des Cuisiniers*. Paris: Éditions LT Jacques Lanore, 2004, pp. 100–101.

Ranhofer, Charles. *The Epicurean*. New York: Dover Publications, 1971; reprint of 1893 original work, pp. 1–168.

Strong, Roy. *Feast: A History of Grand Eating*. Copyright Oman Productions 2002. Orlando: Harcourt, Inc., pp. 73–127.

Wheaton, Barbara Ketcham. *Savoring the Past: the French Kitchen and Table from 1300 to 1789*. New York: Touchstone Book edition, published by Simon & Schuster, 1996, pp. 1–94; 138–148; 173–192.

Wilson, C. Anne. "Ritual, Form, and Color in the Mediaeval Food Tradition." Wilson, C. Anne, ed. *The Appetite and the Eye: Visual Aspects of Food and Its Presentation within Their Historic Context*. Second Leeds Symposium on Food History and Traditions, April 1987, with additional papers. Edinburgh: Edinburgh University Press, 1991, pp. 5–27.

Wilson, C. Anne. "Ideal Meals and Their Menus from the Middle Ages to the Georgian Era." C. Anne Wilson, ed. *The Appetite and the Eye: Visual Aspects of Food and Its Presentation within Their Historic Context*. Second Leeds Symposium on Food History and Traditions, April 1987, with additional papers. Edinburgh: Edinburgh University Press, 1991, pp. 98–122.

Images

Carter, Charles. *The Complete Practical Cook*. London: Printed for W. Meadows, C. Rivington; and R. Hett, 1730, pp. 24, 51. Courtesy Lilly Library, Indiana University, Bloomington, Indiana.

Dubois, Urbain, and Emile Bernard. *La Cuisine Classique études pratiques, raisonnées et de l'école Française appliqué au service a la russe*. Paris: Chez Les Auteurs, 1856. Volume 1: Plate #3, Plate #10. Courtesy Lilly Library, Indiana University, Bloomington, Indiana.

Gilliers, Sieur. *Le cannameliste française*. 1758. Nancy: Chez Jean-Baptiste-Hiacinthe Leclerc; et Paris: Chez Merlin 1768, pp. 230. Courtesy Lilly Library, Indiana University, Bloomington, Indiana.

Wauquelin, Jean. *Livre des Conquestes et faits d'Alexandre*. *~1448*. Courtesy Petit Palais, Musée des Beaux-Arts de la Ville de Paris inventory number: LDUT00456. Folio 86 recto (image number: 40153-4).

4

Platter to Plate:
Classical Style

In the last chapter, *Frames* were established for three types of service and their attendant menus within the category of artistic dining. The foundation of artistic dining in the United States was established as part of the French tradition. Before continuing to the *Plate Frame,* Classical cuisine needs to be better situated within the system being developed in this book.

◎ BACKGROUND

We have been considering Professional cuisine as it is practiced as part of an increasingly global network but with our focus being the United States. So, when chefs refer to *Classical cuisine,* are they referring to a separate, different cuisine? The answer is no, not in the new system being developed in this book. Classical becomes a style within Professional cuisine. Traditionally, culinary commenters, not chefs, named the professional styles of cooking. For reasons of clarity, this book changes the way of labeling different practices that have become part of Professional cuisine.

People who write about food, such as food critics or gastronomes, notice changes in general practices and then set about to describe and label them. However, styles are retroactive. They are not established as theories that are then applied to practice but, rather, they are criteria extrapolated out of practice to explain ways of working that are similar. These labels often become absorbed by a culinary community, which then either affirms or disavows that it is part of such a movement.

For example, the style of aristocratic dining that took place in wealthy households is sometimes referred to as *Grande* cuisine, while *Haute* cuisine is the same style translated into restaurant service. Both "cuisines" are being ranked within French cuisine, which also contains branches such as Bourgeois, regional, Nouvelle, and Classic. However, these are not separate cuisines for a chef but rather are styles within Professional cuisine. To make this more obvious, consider French chefs whose work personifies Grande cuisine, such as Antonin Carême and Urbain Dubois. Both chefs worked with *service à la française* and *service à la russe*. Both chefs would probably have thought of their practice as belonging to Classical cuisine, as can be seen in the title of Chef Dubois' cookbook: *La Cuisine classique, études pratique, raisonnées et demonstratives de l'école française appliqué au service à la Russe*, with Émile Bernard 1856. Yet at the same time, they sometimes referred to their work as being part of the Nouvelle cuisine—in all likelihood, because they felt they were progressing into new territory (Dubois 1856).

The use of such labels as *nouvelle* (which has been used more than once in the French tradition) or *avant-garde* to describe styles is not the best practice because there is always something new or cutting edge later. As I develop the Plate Frame, I will suggest alternate names for styles within Professional cuisine to better delineate what is being discussed. For our purposes, Grande "cuisine" is a foundational methodology for Professional cuisine. And, from our viewpoint, Classical "cuisine," again, really a style within Professional cuisine, is defined by the work of Chef Auguste Escoffier.

FIGURE 4.1

Tournedos Rossini, a Classical Dish. Tournedos are small steaks cut from the beef tenderloin; for Rossini, they are garnished with foie gras and truffles.

Gisslen, Wayne. *Professional Cooking, 7th Edition*. Hoboken, New Jersey: Copyright © 2011 by John Wiley & Sons, Inc. Reprinted with permission of John Wiley & Sons, Inc.

◎ CLASSICAL STYLE

When something is called a classic, it implies that thing is the finest example of its kind. It is the acknowledged standard of quality and value: an archetype that generally defines what is considered elegance within an area of design. Classical things hold enduring significance. Classical style in Professional cuisine has endured for over a century; its menu structure and service style are still in use today. That is why Escoffier's *Le Guide Culinaire*, which was first published in 1903, continues to be in print today (OED 2011, "classic").

The flavor associations in Classical dishes remain a strong influence for how flavors are currently associated. For example, think of the *Mother sauces*. Sauce Hollandaise is still paired with steaks and asparagus; similarly, consider the flavor associations of

Canard à l'Orange. The dishes of the Classical repertoire are still produced and still inspire chefs to reproduce them in newer versions. However, to work in the Classical style is very different than the way most chefs work today. A Classical chef does not seek to improvise or create dishes, but rather to exhibit perfect control in producing dishes that are part of the established repertoire. For this reason, menus were written in a language that was codified by the Classical repertoire. Dishes have standardized ingredients and names of dishes refer to the garnishes used on the platter or in the sauce. These names were originally given based on the location of the inspiration, such as *à la Normande*, or referred to a famous patron for whom the dish was originally created (Escoffier 1982).

Louis Saulnier, a student of Escoffier, published in 1914 *Le Repertoire de la Cuisine* as a memory aid for skilled cooks. In the introduction he writes:

> *This question of names deserves the closest attention for it seems full of pitfalls. Almost every day some well-intentioned chef or cook will either give a new name to a dish which is already known to everyone as something else or he will introduce under a well-known name a preparation different from that which the name normally implies. These are bad practices which all chefs and cooks conscious of their professional responsibility should do their best to stamp out. If allowed to continue, such practices will debase the culinary art beyond redemption (Saulnier 1976, vii).*

In *Le Guide*, recipes are written in a culinary shorthand for established cooks. *Le Repertoire* offers even less direction; there are not really recipes but rather one-line descriptions of a dish's elements. For example, to know what is in the dish Filet Sole Bonne Femme, the cook would look up "sole, Bonne-Femme" and follow the definitions:

Sole Bonne-Femme: Same as Boitelle, with a border of sliced steamed potatoes.

Sole Boitelle: Same as Bercy, with the addition of sliced mushrooms.

Sole Bercy: Poached with shallots and chopped parsley, white wine and fish stock. Reduce the stock, add butter, and coat the fish, glaze (Saulnier 1976, 97).

The codification of dishes was very important in Classical style. Both *Le Guide* and *Le Repertoire* are divided according to how the dishes would fit into a classical menu. Saulnier's 1914 *Répertoire* contained about 2,000 more dishes than Escoffier's 1903 *Le Guide Culinaire*, which contains just over 5,000 recipes; this shows continual development in the classical repertoire. Esteemed chefs from different European countries or the United States, who created dishes that received enough acclaim, would standardize the dish. These international dishes were added into the French repertoire and formed a style referred to as *Continental,* practiced in many of the large, luxurious hotels and restaurants in the first half of the twentieth century.

Neither of these books contains pictures or photographs because cooking traditions were passed from hand to eye through practice. Learning the techniques and methods of cookery was primary, and the look of the food was embedded in these practices.

THE CLASSICAL MENU AND SERVICE

Menu

The early menu sequence of à la carte artistic dining is still extensive compared to today's standards; its series generally consisted of 10 to 12 courses. The following is a typical example of a menu sequence extrapolated from Escoffier's menus:

Example of Courses in an Escoffier Menu

Course Name	Example of Dish Served in the Course	Description
Cold hors d'oeuvre	Huîtres Natives au Caviar (#966)	small tartlets, garnished with caviar, topped with a fresh oyster
Soup	Consommé Madrilène (#569)	Clear broth, garnished with diced tomato and pimento
Fish (Hot Hors d'oeuvre)	Paupiette de Sole Orientale (#1995)	stuffed, rolled sole filets with lobster sauce lightly flavored with curry; garnish of cooked lobster meat; served with rice
Relevé	Côtelette de volaille à la Maréchale (#3156)	airline breast of chicken standard breading; pan fried in clarified butter; topped with truffle slice; center of platter garnished with buttered asparagus tips
Entrée	Noisette d'agneau Rachel (#447)	lamb tenderloin or eye of loin; artichoke bottoms garnished with poached bone marrow and parsley; sauce Bordelaise
Punch	Punch glace (#5009)	granite of sauterne and tea flavored with lemon, orange, and rum
Roast	Caille au raisin (#3687)	quails in a casserole with peeled, seeded grapes
(Salad with Roast)	Cœurs de Romaine	hearts of Romaine lettuce
Cold Dish	Parfait de foie gras (#3519)	cold, molded pâté of foie gras
Entremets, sweet	Pêches Alexandra (#4667)	vanilla poached peaches, arranged on top of vanilla ice cream, coated with strawberry puree, sprinkled with red & white rose petals, and covered with a veil of spun sugar
Dessert	Friandises	iced petit fours
Coffee and Liquors		

The center column in the Escoffier example menu is the way the menu items would have been written. Look at the type of language that is used to present the idea of what the dish is to the customer. Diners were expected to be knowledgeable about the classical repertoire. Their choices depended on being able to recognize that when something is called "Rachel," artichoke bottoms garnished with bone marrow will be part of the dish. There was an understanding shared between the diner and the chef that created a dining culture.

Notice that the hot food sequence is bracketed by cold courses; for example, the foie gras is served after the main course of Roasts. This places a very rich dish closer to dessert than the opening of the meal. In the sampling of menus in *Le Guide*, cheese is rarely noted as a course. There are cheese dishes, such as soufflé or gnocchi with cheese, suggested; these generally replace the cold course. If cheese is served, it would mostly likely be included in the dessert offerings with fresh fruit. What we call dessert would have been the sweet entremets course.

The friandises, which are small, one-bite iced cakes, would then move down a course with coffee. Mignardises, the term most often used today, are also a type of petit fours: Small bite-size sweets, like cookies, which are at the end of the meal.

Vegetables are attendant dishes that serve as garnishes with the dominant food. Garnishes—which would appear to be of essential importance because they "name" the dish—are, in reality, secondary to the central food. They are a way of embellishing to increase variety and novelty. These are not add-on sprigs of herbs and such but are, rather, the side dishes accompanying the focus food. Here, we see how the idea of garnishing is moving away from simply decorative ornate elements to functional food constructions. Vegetables are cooked in decorated molds, cut into regular shapes, or held together by vegetable containers. In classical style, garnishes must be edible.

Another precept of Classical style is that the flavor of each course should not be more dominant than the following course; flavor should build from light to more substantial in the order of courses, until the salad. In fact, there should be no strong flavor used in any course that would disrupt the steady rhythm of flavors. Certain ingredients are used to denote value such as truffles, lobster, and foie gras. Foods are chosen in this period not only for their quality but also for their rarity and expense. Also, no ingredient should be repeated in the menu, except perhaps for truffles. The dominant food in a course is generally an animal protein.

In the sample Escoffier menu, there are three meat offerings: chicken, lamb, and then quail. It is typical in classical menus to have three meat courses. The chef would have started with the lightest meats, moving to the heaviest in flavor. If a red meat is offered in one course, the next should be a white meat; meat should vary from course to course. Sauces, too, should vary in color from course to course; a brown sauce should not be followed by a brown sauce in the next course.

Examples of Factors that Affect the "Weight" of Flavors	Cooking Method	Use of Spices or Sauces	Choice of Focus Food
Heavier	Fried	Barbeque sauce	Wild game
	Roasted	Tomato sauce	Chicken
Lighter	Poached	Velouté	Halibut

Service

The menu items were served by wait staff, working from a guéridon tableside. The food was prepared and presented on platters and copper serviceware. The wait staff might

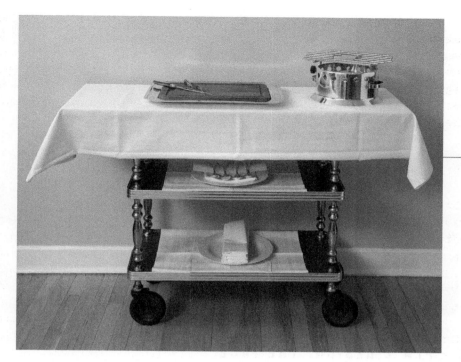

FIGURE 4.2

Guéridon Service. This is an image of a *service* trolley. The trolley would be rolled next to the customer's table where the server would finish preparations of the meal before plating it. The kitchen staff would be responsible for preparing the platter and any necessary accompaniments.

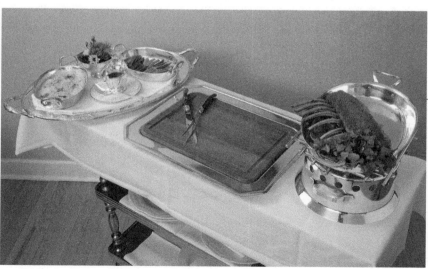

FIGURE 4.3

The Kitchen's Preparations for Tableside Service of Lamb Chops. This image shows the platters and accompaniments sent from the kitchen on the service trolley. Presented here is a rack of lamb with vegetables, potatoes, and sauce.

finish a preparation, such as carving or deboning, and move the food to a plate for an individual diner.

Thus, the first plate design began in the *Platter Frame,* where chefs dressed mostly platters and service vessels to be sent to the dining room, and wait staff, not chefs, decided on the placement of the foods on the plate.

Plating Tableside. This image shows a waiter preparing to plate the lamb chops, vegetables, and potatoes tableside.

◎ PLATE DESIGN: THE FACE

Often, servers used the most straightforward of plate designs, resembling a **Face**.

This design presents a meat, one starch, and one vegetable. Occasionally, there is a second vegetable; additionally, there is sometimes only a meat and one side dish, presented side by side.

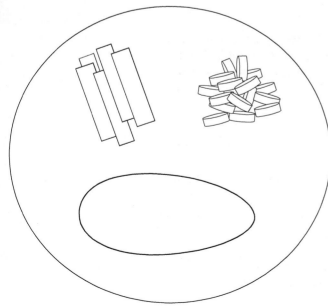

When placing the dishes onto the plate, there are rules to be followed; for example:

◆ The focus food is always placed closest to the diner.

◆ If a bone of any kind is to be left on meat, the bone must point away from the dinner.

◆ Hot food must be piping hot and served on hot plates.

◆ Cold foods are served on chilled plates.

◆ Temperatures do not mix on the plate and generally do not mix within the same course.

The Face plate presents flavors in a way that allows the diner to choose in what order the dishes will be eaten and if they will be commingled. Therefore, each dish must be complete in itself, yet the flavor(s) of each dish must complement the other two dishes. For example, if one of the dishes is *Gratin Dauphinois*, which is creamy with milk and cheese, it would not be complementary to serve *Haricots Verts à la Tourangelle*, which are cooked green beans in a Béchamel sauce. The sauce for the potatoes is not flattered by the sauce for the green beans; instead, the two are competing.

Sauces blanket almost all foods except fried dishes. Generally, the sauce choice flows from the cooking method. White sauces are not used with dry-heat cooking methods. Cooking methods, recognized as moist-heat versus dry-heat categories, are not to be mixed in one course, except for the element of pastry. In other words, if a fish is poached, then any attendant garnishes or sauce garnishes should be cooked by a moist-heat method as well. A roasted bird would not be paired with mashed potatoes, a moist-heat method, but with potatoes cooked using a dry-heat method, such as sautéed potatoes. Although textures might vary, no texture should be sharply contrasted with other textures, except in one small element, such as a pastry crust or crouton. Creamy and smooth are considered the best textures for Classical dishes.

The Blue Plate Special

The Face plate is a fundamental design that is used across all sectors of service—from diners to artistic dining—as well as at home. It is the basic pattern for family-style meals in diners and coffee-shops, which traditionally consisted of a meat and two side dishes. In U.S. diners, during the first half of the 1900s, this type of meal was often served in a divided plate and called a *Blue Plate Special*. In the 1950s, when frozen TV dinners were first being produced, they had the same design but in a heatable aluminum divided tray (OED 2011, "blue-plate") (see Color Image 1).

This manual will trace the process in *culinary Art history* of moving from the Face plate to a more complicated plate design without losing the fundamental flavors of the dishes being served. This reflects the underlying question of how food can be presented artistically without losing its primary focus of flavor.

◎ MAJOR TENETS OF CLASSICAL STYLE

◆ Symmetry is necessary in platter arrangements. Each side must match exactly in number and shape of food items.

◆ Geometric shapes are used to mold vegetables and starches. Heaps, piles, and scatters are not acceptable. Food is not to be too closely associated with its natural form.

◆ Service personnel are as much a part of the artistic display of food as the cooks.

◆ Menus are written in a language that is codified by the Classical repertoire. Dishes have standardized ingredients.

- Names of dishes refer to the garnishes used on the platter or in the sauce.

- Sauces blanket almost all foods. Sauces should vary in color from course to course.

- Generally, the sauce choice flows from the cooking method. For instance, white sauces are not generally used with dry-heat cooking methods.

- Cooking methods, recognized as moist-heat versus dry-heat categories, are not to be mixed in one course, except for the element of pastry.

- Garnish is a concept fundamental to this style. Garnishes are often the vegetable side dishes that accompany the dominant food or elements put into a sauce.

- Garnishes must be functional, never inedible.

- Although textures might vary, no texture should be sharply contrasted with other textures, except in one small element, such as a pastry crust or crouton. Creamy and smooth are considered best.

- There should be no strong flavor used in any course that would disrupt the steady rhythm of flavors.

- The flavor of each course should not be more dominant than the following course.

- Flavors are not to be isolated but blended; in each course, the flavors should be harmonized so that none are dominant.

- Hot and cold foods are not paired in the same course, except for peeled fruit, tender herb sprigs, or watercress bouquets, used as garnishes.

- No ingredient should be repeated in the menu, except perhaps for truffles.

- The dominant food in a course is generally animal protein, which should vary from course to course; a red meat should be followed by a white meat, or vice versa.

- Temperatures should not be contrasted within a course or too sharply between courses.

- Hot food is served on hot plates and cold foods on chilled plates.

QUERIES & INQUIRIES

1. What do the terms *Grande cuisine* and *Haute cuisine* mean?
2. What printed work defines *Classical style* for the professional chef in the United States?
3. How do chefs work differently today compared to a chef working in the classical style?
4. How are menu items described in Classical style?
5. What is garnishing for a Classical chef? Where are garnishes used?

QUERIES & INQUIRIES *Continued*

6. When executing a Classical menu, what is the flavor pattern?

7. How are most dishes presented to the customer in a Classical menu service?

8. This inquiry will be developed in Chapters 4 through 8. There is an example of the completed exercise in the color inset of this manual built on #2414 Pièce de Boeuf à la Bourguignonne. (See Color Images 6–15.)

   Using Escoffier's *Le Guide Culinaire* choose a *dish* that would now be considered a main course. The choice you make is important as you will need to use the same ingredients or flavors to continue this inquiry in the following chapters. Good places to begin are in the sections on Filet de Boeuf (Fillet of Beef), starting with recipe number 2234, or Tournedos of Beef, starting with recipe number 2298.

   After carefully choosing the Classical *dish*, either draw or cook the presentation. Write a menu description in Classical style language. If you have the opportunity to cook the *dish*, document your work with a photograph.

   a. What are your thoughts about the *dish*?
   b. Does this style of presentation express the desired flavors clearly?
   c. If you have cooked the *dish*, describe what eating it was like. Did the forms correspond to what you think of as food?

CITATION AND REFERENCE MATERIALS

"blue, adj." "blue-plate, n US." OED Online. March 2011. Oxford University Press. Retrieved April 4, 2011, at www.oed.com/view/Entry/20577.

"classic, adj. and n." OED Online. March 2011. Oxford University Press. Retrieved April 4, 2011, at www.oed.com/view/Entry/33880?redirectedFrom=classic.

Claiborne, Craig, and Pierre Franey, and the editors of TIME-LIFE Books. *Classic French Cooking*. New York: Time-Life Books, 1970.

Dubois, Urbain, and Emile Bernard. *La Cuisine Classique études pratiques, raisonnées et de l'école Française appliqué au service a la russe*. Paris: Chez Les Auteurs, 1856.

Escoffier, Auguste. *Le Guide Culinaire*. Trans. H. L. Cracknell and R. J. Kaufmann. New York: Mayflower Books, 1982.

Saulnier, Louis. *Le Repertoire de la Cuisine*. New York: Barron's Educational Series, 1976.

Images

Gisslen, Wayne. *Professional Cooking*, 7th ed. Hoboken, New Jersey: John Wiley & Sons, 2011.

5

Plate Frame:
Nouvelle Style

 BACKGROUND

Nouvelle style is a reaction to the Classical approach. Classical style has had long-lasting effects on professional cooking but was most prominent from 1900 to 1960. This period of time encompassed great global changes in culture, politics, and technology. During this period, the world had little time to consider dining as an art form. Nevertheless, throughout this period of platter service, slowly and in small measures, artistic dining was changing as was the Frame of food presentations.

World War I (1914–1919) was like a line drawn between the old and new world. Empires and aristocracies were destroyed; new countries were created. The public celebrated modernity and embraced the luxuries that new technologies could bring them. Art Deco was the design style of the age. Ornamental trimmings were discarded in favor of geometric shapes and clean lines.

The world had briefly recovered from World War I only to again experience terrible suffering and food shortages during the Great Depression and World War II. Following these catastrophes, as life began to return to normal, people felt a renewed optimism and sense of possibility. At the same time, restaurant dining became accessible to more people, and the menu structure used in artistic dining had shortened and shifted, reflecting the trend toward streamline design.

Classical and Continental repertories still defined the dishes being served, but the menu generally consisted of not more than nine courses:

1. Cold hors d'oeuvre
2. Soup
3. Fish
4. Sorbet
5. Meat
6. Salad
7. Cheese
8. Dessert
9. Coffee and friandises or mignardises

This style of menu was dominant in artistic dining in Europe and the United States until the 1970s. The 1960s had been a turbulent time of social unrest and cultural exploration. Chefs correspondingly felt constrained by the codified structure of Classical menus. They began to express themselves in more personalized dishes and, at first, more simplified visual constructions. This shift in artistic dining, credited in large part to the pivotal work of Chef Fernand Point, was to become the Nouvelle "cuisine" of the 1970s and early 1980s.

At the same time, the United States, long thought to be without an independent culinary tradition, began to assert its own style in restaurant and service designs.

Fernand Point (1897–1955) Chef-Owner of La Pyramide in Vienne, France

La Pyramide was among the first restaurants to receive a three-star Michelin rating, which began in the 1930s. Chef Point created what was later called a personal cuisine. Working from his training in Classical cuisine, he created dishes that suited the market, his tastes, and the taste of his customers. Point worked on the perfection of dishes, believing in the freshest and best ingredients prepared fresh every day. He was one of the first chefs to greet customers in the dining room. For Point, "cooking was an accumulation of small details done correctly." He had a great influence in the development of the Nouvelle style, having trained many of its upcoming stars, such as Paul Bocuse and the Troisgros brothers (Point 1969, 52; Blake 1978).

◎ NOUVELLE STYLE: IMPRESSIONISTIC DESIGN

As noted in Chapter 4, the naming of styles with labels such as *nouvelle* or *avant-garde* is not the best practice. As a case in point, in the history of French cooking, there have been at least two other periods of cookery that were labeled nouvelle. Therefore, I would suggest that this latest Nouvelle style would have been better labeled *Impressionistic*.

Chefs working in the Nouvelle style were like the Impressionists. The Impressionists strove to develop painting that, while still being representational like their classical predecessors, styled the elements of the work in a personalized arrangement. Impressionist painters had a deep affinity with nature and tried to express this in new ways of seeing and organizing its appreciation, as did Nouvelle chefs.

Both Nouvelle chefs and Impressionist artists were the last representational styles before the rapid acceleration of change and the development of many diverse movements in their respective mediums. Notice that the Impressionistic expression of food comes about a hundred years after that movement in painting. Culinary aesthetics develop more slowly than Art in relation to changes within general culture; this lag time is present for all *culinary Art* developments as well.

Nouvelle "cuisine" was defined by two French restaurant critics, Henri Gault and Christian Millau. Their ten criteria of Nouvelle style have been translated and interpreted in many different ways; however, the application of these changes was most important in relation to Classical style. At first, Nouvelle chefs still took their inspiration from Classical foundations but reorganized its elements into a more personalized expression.

FIGURE 5.1

Salmon with Sorrel Sauce. This is an image of *Salmon à l'Oseille*, an iconic Nouvelle plate. Notice that there is no ornamentation on this plate, representative of the beginnings of Nouvelle style, simply salmon and sorrel sauce. The creation of this dish is generally attributed to Chefs Pierre and Jean Troisgros.

The Original Ten Criteria of Nouvelle Style

Gault and Millau, while researching restaurants, began to notice that some chefs were cooking dishes that were outside of the Classical repertoire, a repertoire that they felt had become hackneyed. Their first introduction to this style took place at Chef Paul Bocuse's restaurant, who then recommended that they visit Chefs Jean and Pierre Troisgros. Through continued examination of this new trend, they came to write a ten-point list that defined the characteristics of this style:

1. Refuse unnecessary complications. Simplicity is better than pretentious names and presentations.

2. Reduce cooking times for most fish, crustaceans, duck, roast game, veal, certain green vegetables, and noodles; rediscover the steam cooking method.

3. Let the cooking be directed by the market. Buy your products fresh daily and chose what the world has yet to spoil.

4. Do not have an overly extensive à la carte menu. The food will be fresher and the cooking less routine.

5. Do not age or marinate game.

6. Refuse to use rich, heavy sauces like *espagnoles* and *béchamels*. Use natural juices, small amounts of cream, and fresh herbs. Use clear, light sauces like beurre blanc. Also, do not use cheese to gratin the tops of dishes.

7. Return to regional cuisines and family recipes for inspiration.

8. Be curious about new techniques. Use new technologies, such as microwaves.

9. Think about a healthy diet. Work with lighter dishes, salads, simply cooked fresh vegetables, and rarer meats.

10. Be creative. There remain thousands of dishes to invent and surely a couple hundred to retain.

(Author's translation) (Gault 1976, 154–157)

Chefs now took inspiration from regional, hearth-cuisines, as well as the Professional tradition. Chefs also drew inspiration from the pastry kitchen, creating dishes such as *Millefeuille of Salmon* or *Choux au Foie Gras*. This type of playful appropriation is characteristic of Nouvelle style.

This opened the door to ingredients not found in the classical repertoire, such as basil and pink peppercorns. New, and slightly bolder, flavor combinations were created such as kiwis paired with fish. The goal was to let the natural flavor of the ingredients shine through the cooking processes. Thus, cooking methods such as frying, roasting, and braising become less used, while poaching and steaming become more important. Sauces were lighter in texture to allow natural flavors to be highlighted.

All the food on the plate was to be prepared to reflect a more organic beauty inherent in the ingredients. Shapes were not to be contrived; natural forms of baby vegetables, or minimally cut and cooked vegetables, were used to create design patterns. If any molding of foods was done, it was predominately done to starches without detracting from their ideal texture. Figurative shapes, such as cups made from vegetables, were to be avoided as old fashioned and unnatural.

Vegetables played a much more important role on Nouvelle plates than in Classical menus. Despite the fact that in the classical repertoire, dishes were often named by their vegetable accompaniments, chefs and diners focused on the animal protein of the plate. Nouvelle chefs gave greater status to vegetables, using more in proportion to the protein focus food.

Part of this new creative process changed the way a chef thought about garnishes. At first all garnishes were removed to achieve a purity of expression; the only added garnish might have been sprigs of chervil. Later, items were added predominantly for their visual effect, much like jewelry on an outfit. Things like savory tuiles, fried julienne or spiral-cut vegetables, vegetable chips, and fried herbs all added visual interest, as well as flavor.

Value in Classical dishes was embedded in luxury ingredients like truffles. Nouvelle chefs still appreciated such luxury items, but value was denoted by market-fresh ingredients, especially baby vegetables, as well as the stylization or look of the plates.

Now, plates were more elaborately styled than any service staff had time to accomplish in the dining room. As a result, the creative work of a chef was now directly perceived by a diner. Thus, the chef became a personality, replacing the status previously held by the restaurant owner or maître d'hôtel.

FIGURE 5.2

Millefeuille of Salmon. A Millefeuille is typically dessert, sometimes called a Napoleon, consisting of three layers of puff pastry and two layers of cream. The top is often glazed with white icing and chocolate stripes or dusted with powdered sugar. Here, the Nouvelle chef has turned the pastry model into a savory creation using puff pastry and salmon.

This was one of the most important changes brought about by Nouvelle practitioners: the blurring of the difference between *dish* creation and *plate* construction. Chefs working in Classical menus repeated standardized accompaniments in prescribed shapes and arranged in limited acceptable patterns. Nouvelle chefs were more likely to choose accompaniments that not only added flavor to the dish but also, and just as importantly, enhanced the look of the plate. *Dishes* were now visual because they centered around plate construction. Plating had evolved into another way of creating a *dish*.

Spa "cuisine" is another style of Professional cuisine that began developing alongside Nouvelle style. It shares the philosophy of lighter sauces, reduced portion size, and fresh, simply cooked ingredients. Michel Guérard, a prominent Nouvelle chef, was pivotal in creating the Spa style. He developed a "cuisine of slimness" called *Cuisine Minceur*. The point was to prepare healthful, low-calorie dishes that would please a sophisticated palate. Chefs, such as Seppi Renggli at the Four Seasons hotel in New York, furthered the style at spas and hotels (Guérard 1976; Renggli 1986).

◉ THE NOUVELLE MENU AND SERVICE

Menu

The Nouvelle menu was no longer written in a language based on the concept of garnish but rather on ingredients. Often, visually complex dishes were named after hearth-cuisine dishes or pastry constructions, forming a playful sophistication within the style. Examples of such dishes are:

◆ Millefeuille de Saumon (Salmon Napoleon)

◆ Charlotte d'Agneau (Lamb Mousse filled with Lamb Stew)

◆ Ravioli Ouvert aux Asperges (Open Ravioli with Asparagus)

While Nouvelle menus were still often structured to the nine Classical courses, abbreviated sequences were gaining popularity. It was not unusual to find menus reduced to five courses:

1. Appetizer
2. (Entrée) Main course
3. Salad

4. Cheese
5. Dessert

> FIGURE 5.3
>
> **"Open" Ravioli.** These differ from the traditional presentation in two significant ways. The ravioli are not sealed pasta packages, but rather a stacked presentation of filling between two sheets of pasta; and, instead of a number of ravioli being presented on a plate to comprise the dish, there is generally only one open ravioli presented.

This menu sequence is close to the American style:

◆ Appetizer: fruit cup, juice, seafood cocktail, melon, canapé, oyster or clams

◆ Soup

◆ Salad

◆ Main course with potato and vegetable

◆ Dessert

The overall effect of such a menu was lightness and brightness, expressed in smaller, stylized food arrangements. "Naturalness that was not natural"—that was the value this period expressed by subtly staging the highest quality of market produce available.

Service

One characteristic that should have been part of the original list of ten criteria is this:

Chefs should plate food in the kitchen; food should not be plated by service staff in the dining room.

Now, service personnel participated only marginally in the presentation of food; the cooks in the kitchen entirely controlled the placement of food on plates. Thus, the service used in Nouvelle style is all American. In the United States, chefs had long been plating food in the kitchen, but artistic dining had previously followed the French model of *service au guéridon*. With the Nouvelle style, artistic dining switched to the American à la carte service.

Another difference in Nouvelle presentations was the size of the plate. Serving portions in Nouvelle style were often criticized as being too small to satisfy an appetite. This might have been the case in some instances, but the general misperception of the portion size is key to understanding this criticism. The plating that had gone on before in U.S. restaurants was basically the face design, served on about 9-inch dinner plates. In Nouvelle style, not only did the presentation design change but also the size of the plate increased to about 12 inches. Plating in the kitchen and the use of large, minimally decorated plates was revolutionary in artistic dining.

Elements of the Nouvelle Plate

Sauces, a defining characteristic of Professional cuisine, became a design element. One of the tenets of Nouvelle cuisine was to eliminate flour-thickened sauces. This led to less viscous liquids, which did not have the same potential to coat foods. As well, the color of sauces became more luminous, brighter. Previously derived from the focus food of meat or fish, Nouvelle sauces became more independent. Emulsified butter sauces and vegetable coulis were used extensively. Sauces of all kinds were used to draw patterns of dotting or dragging and even pictures.

Also, the secondary food elements were less manipulated than in the Classical garnishes, striving to reflect a more natural appearance. The use of baby vegetables highlighted this period's value of presenting "nature." Starches, on the other hand,

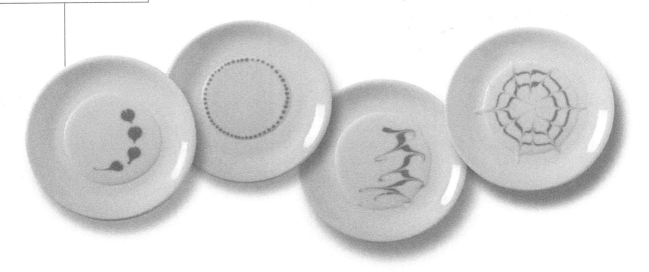

were still generally shaped or molded. The dominant food was still one of meat, fish, or game, as in the Classical menu, but the vegetables and starches were becoming more important.

When Nouvelle style began, the presentations were very straightforward, much like *dishes* would be served at home. As manipulations on the plate increased, fanning and shingling slices augmented visual impact. Whereas before, large roasts were sliced to portion, on Nouvelle plates individual portions of meat were sliced and laid out. Subsequently, vegetables were also sliced and used to create circles or flat background color fields.

◎ PLATE DESIGN: THE SUN

The first pattern of food placement done entirely by chefs in the kitchen resembled a sun. The second variation might even be called **the Sun Bug**, but that might sound slightly unappetizing. The sauce was no longer used to cover, but rather to create a background. Generally placed in a ring around the central item, the secondary elements radiated out on top of the sauce field.

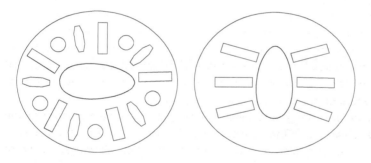

◎ PLATE DESIGN: THE FAN

These patterns of food placement resemble a fan. The other vegetables/starches radiate from the top of focus foods. The sauce is semi-circled at the bottom of the plate providing weight to this half of the plate.

◎ PLATE DESIGN: ISLAND(S)

One source of inspiration for new dishes came from the Classical repertoire of desserts. Napoleons of foie gras, pâte à choux with a brandade filling, or lamb charlottes became focus items on plates. These foods were often presented as an island or islands in sauce. Diners had less control over the order in which dishes on the plate were eaten. Instead, the construction of the plate guided how flavors were perceived.

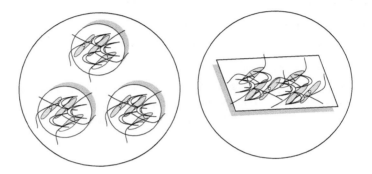

◎ MAJOR TENETS OF NOUVELLE STYLE

- ◆ Creativity is essential. Use all the previous development of dishes in the classical repertoire, in pastry, and in home-cooking as a springboard to create new presentations of these flavors and forms.

- ◆ The freshest ingredients from the market should guide your dishes' development.

- ◆ Traditional *dishes* can be taken apart and their elements restylized into components of a Nouvelle plate, arranging them in layers, circles, or rays on the plate. The nascent idea of deconstruction begins.

- ◆ Symmetrical designs are best.

- ◆ Circular arrangements or fans of slices are common. These techniques lighten texture, while providing a visual complexity.

- ◆ Sauces should be used as a background to foods; avoid blanketing foods with sauce.

- ◆ More than one sauce can be used to heighten color in the design. Dotting, drawing, and dragging sauces into other sauces increase visual interest.

- ◆ Beurre blanc is the new "mother" sauce.

- ◆ Superfluous garnishes should be removed. Stylize ingredients to elevate them into professional cuisine.

- ◆ Figurative forming of foods is old-fashioned. Do not use contrived shapes.

◆ If any molding is done, it should be kept to a minimum and the texture of the food, generally a starch, should not be compromised.

◆ The natural colors of vegetables and herbs should be used to brighten plates; de-emphasize meat colors.

◆ Portion sizes should be smaller.

◆ Empty space is very important on the plate; it provides greater focus to the food on the plate.

◆ Vegetables and seafood of all kinds, not only shellfish, are elevated in status.

◆ The natural textures and flavors of ingredients must be respected; textures such as crispness of vegetables and *mi-cuit* (half-cooked) fish are valued.

◆ Cooking times and grinding of foods should be minimized.

◆ The use of stronger flavor elements, such as herbs and aromatics (garlic, onion), should not be muted as in Classical style but drawn from regional, home-based traditions.

◆ Poaching and steaming should be used whenever possible.

◆ The menu should be shortened. Fewer courses, featuring more clearly articulated flavors, should build in steady intensity to the salad. Lighter meats should come before darker meats.

◆ The menu should no longer be written in a language based on the concept of garnish, but rather on ingredients used on the plate.

◆ Playful sophistication, referencing older dishes or pastries, in the naming of menu items exhibits a chef's creativity.

QUERIES & INQUIRIES

1. What are the nine courses listed for a formal meal after World War II?

2. Why can Nouvelle style be compared to Impressionist art? Is *Nouvelle* the best name for this style?

3. What two French food writers helped to define Nouvelle style in the 1970s?

4. What is Spa style, and how does it differ from Nouvelle style?

5. How is the Nouvelle written menu different from the Classical written menu?

6. What are the changes in service from Classical to Nouvelle style?

7. What elements become important on Nouvelle plates?

8. How is the visual embellishment of the plate achieved? How are Nouvelle plates garnished?

QUERIES & INQUIRIES   *Continued*

9. What are the archetypal plate designs in Nouvelle?

10. What are the tenets of Nouvelle style?

11. Who are well-known chefs that developed and worked in Nouvelle style?

12. Using the Classical dish that you had chosen for the inquiry in Chapter 4, re-plate the ingredients and flavors to match the archetypal plate designs provided in this chapter. This can be done in the kitchen or through drawing. Write a menu description in the new style's language.

If you have the opportunity to cook the *dish,* document your work with a photograph.

   a. What are your thoughts about the *dish*?
   b. Does this style of presentation express the desired flavors clearly?
   c. If you have cooked the *dish,* describe what eating it was like. Did the forms correspond to what you think of as food?
   d. Did the re-presentation of flavors change the taste of the *dish*? Was it an improvement?

CITATION AND REFERENCE MATERIALS

Blake, Anthony, and Quentin Crewe. *Great Chefs of France.* New York: Galley Press, 1978.

Bocus, Paul. *La Cuisine du Marche.* France: Flammarion, 1976.

Brenner, Leslie. *American Appetite.* New York: HarperCollins Publishers, Inc., 1999.

"Historique." Gault & Millau Trouver le Meilleur; Toujours. 2010. Retrieved April 4, 2011, at www.gault millau.fr/history.jsp.

Gault, Henri, and Christian Millau. *Gault et Millau se mettent à table.* Paris: Stock, 1976.

Gault-Millau. *Dining in France.* New York: Stewart, Tabori & Chang, 1986.

Goss, Jared. "Design, 1900–25." In *Heilbrunn Timeline of Art History.* New York: The Metropolitan Museum of Art, 2000–(October 2004). Retrieved April 4, 2011, at www.metmuseum.org/toah/hd/dsgn1/hd_dsgn1.htm.

Griffith Winton, Alexandra. "The Bauhaus, 1919–1933". In *Heilbrunn Timeline of Art History.* New York: The Metropolitan Museum of Art, 2000–(August 2007).

Retrieved April 4, 2011, at www.metmuseum.org/toah/hd/bauh/hd_bauh.htm.

Guérard, Michel. *Cuisine Minceur.* New York: William Morrow & Co, 1976.

Mennell, Stephen. *All Manners of Food.* 2nd ed. Chicago: University of Illinois Press, 1996.

Point, Fernand. *Ma Gastronomie.* Paris: Flammarion, 1969.

Renggli, Seppi. *The Four Seasons Spa Cuisine.* New York: Simon & Schuster, 1986.

Troisgros, Jean. *The Nouvelle Cuisine of Jean & Pierre Troisgros.* New York: William Morrow & Co, translation 1978.

"The United States and Canada, 1900 A.D.–present." In *Heilbrunn Timeline of Art History.* New York: The Metropolitan Museum of Art, 2000–(October 2004). Retrieved April 4, 2011, at www.metmuseum.org/toah/ht/?period=11®ion=na.

Urvater, Michele. *Cooking the Nouvelle Cuisine in America.* New York: Workman, 1979.

6

Plate Frame:
New American Style and Fusion Style

 ## BACKGROUND

The idea of what a chef was or did changed dramatically with Nouvelle style. Except for a few celebrated chefs, cooks throughout history were considered similar to domestic help. Chefs and cooks struggled to be recognized as part of a profession. A number of influences came together during the 1960s and 1970s that made this possible. Nouvelle style bought the chef out of the kitchen and into the dining room to be recognized as the creator of dishes. Nouvelle chefs also were more likely to be chef-owners rather than hired help, becoming famous as individuals. Media, with its capabilities of color photography, publishing, and television, helped spotlight the achievement of chefs. Coffee-table books, more to be looked at than cooked from, with their large, artfully photographed food, began being published in increasing numbers. Chefs became television personalities, watched as much for entertainment as cooking know-how. This change in the status of chefs was officially recognized in 1976, the year of the American bicentennial. At that time, efforts by the American Culinary Federation resulted in changing the title of executive chef from the service to the professional category in the U.S. Department of Labor's Dictionary of Official Titles (American Culinary Federation 2008).

Simultaneously, the very nature of dining out was changing. Whereas initially people only ate away from home for certain celebrations or due to their work location, now people ate out as a form of entertainment and exploration. The traditional form of fine dining, with its formal manners and protocol, experienced a shift toward a more relaxed atmosphere. Fine dining transformed into artistic dining, where the emphasis was not on class standing but rather on the experience of a chef's work.

Upper-end restaurants had traditionally received their status from ratings by eminent critics or guides. This, too, was changing in the 1980s, which was demonstrated by the increasing importance of the Zagat guides, first published for New York City in 1979. The Zagat guide, unlike other restaurant rating systems, relied on popular opinion sent in from diners rather than the expert critic (Zagat guide 2011).

The United States had also changed its immigration laws during the 1960s, becoming more inclusive of non-Western Europeans, and by the mid-seventies, restaurants from a multitude of different food-ways could be found in big cities. In addition, familiar European cuisines were now being explored with more authentic eyes. For example, Italian food, long stereotyped as meatballs and spaghetti or pizza, became more sophisticated, differentiating between cooking regions of Italy. This deeper interest in Italian food, coupled with Nouvelle chef's interest in making fresh pasta, led to the creation of such dishes as Pasta Primavera, generally attributed to the New York restaurant Le Cirque in the mid-seventies (Lovegren 1995, 323; Brenner 1999).

In 1969, Richard Nixon was the first American president to visit China in 20 years, spurring a renewed, and more sophisticated, interest in Chinese cooking, introducing into Professional cuisine new cooking techniques like red braising and stir-frying. In general, greater ease of air-travel and more accessible information broadened horizons for both chefs and diners in regards to the vast array of ethnic cuisines.

> The adjective *American* does in fact refer to both the North and South continents; but throughout this book I have used the word American to mean from or pertaining to the United States of America.

Thus, there was no longer one way to look at food or artistic dining. While standardization of food products and convenience of preparation made cooking at home easier than ever before, people were becoming more interested in gourmet cooking. This simultaneous interest, from both ends of the culinary spectrum, was similar to trends in the art world, where Pop Art was being displayed in traditional fine art galleries. Diners were encountering ingredients that were new and exciting to most Americans. Wild mushrooms like morels and chanterelles, edible flowers, fresh instead of dried herbs, avocadoes, and flavored vinegars were innovative flavor possibilities on the New American menu.

Surrealism, an art movement with its beginnings in the 1930s, featured works by such artists as Salvador Dali, who combined styles and subjects not generally found together to create dreamscapes unified on a canvas. A lasting impact of Surrealism was the validity it gave to the expression of the imagination, and this type of new appreciation in art could be seen in the eclectic designs of the 1980s, and in the menus of Fusion style. This sort of freedom in the culinary world led to many exciting new ways of presenting and eating food, but it also made it more difficult for beginning cooks to find their way in an ever-expanding repertoire. Having an *eclectic* style means fusing together elements out of their original contexts; however, if this is done without an understanding of the different original contexts, there is a risk of presenting a muddled jumble.

◎ NEW AMERICAN STYLE

New American chefs looked away from the professional tradition and back to home cooking for inspiration. However, they elevated their homestyle dishes by including luxury ingredients, as can be seen in such offerings as Lobster BLTs and Macaroni and Cheese with Truffles. Concurrently with these developments, chefs in the United States were starting to wonder if there was such a thing as "American cuisine." James Beard, often hailed as the father of American cuisine, was the host of America's first cooking show. It aired on NBC starting in 1946 and was called *I Love to Eat*. However, it wasn't until 1972 that his book, *American Cookery,* was published. American fine dining had always been defined by European standards, but times were now changing. For example, in 1982 the Culinary Institute of America, Hyde Park, opened the *American Bounty Restaurant*, and in 1983, Chef Larry Forgione, a protégé of Beard, opened *An American Place* in New York City (Anderson 1997, 247; The Culinary Institute of America 2011; Forgione 1996).

The New American chef and the Nouvelle French chefs both looked to local markets and regional traditions to create their menus. But most American chefs had not grown up in the French tradition, so as they developed their cooking styles, other backgrounds influenced their food choices. At first they melded these choices with French methodology and techniques, as can be seen in the menu courses and platings based on Nouvelle style. They incorporated French techniques such as mousse and terrine making, and French sauces such as vegetable coulis and beurre blanc, into the presentations of American dishes. For example, a New American appetizer might be Grits Mousse with Shrimp and Beurre Blanc.

FIGURE 6.1

Grits Mousse with Shrimp and Beurre Blanc

California's restaurants became as important as New York's in the culinary world, which led to a style referred to by food writers as *California "cuisine."* The work of chefs such as Alice Waters, Michael McCarty, Jeremiah Towers, and Wolfgang Puck in the 1970s and the 1980s epitomized the California style. Grilling, particularly with mesquite, was the predominant cooking method. Pizzas and salads rose to main course status with the use of unexpected ingredients such as smoked salmon pizza or lobster medallions served on top of field greens. Local ingredients, often organic, were highlighted with Asian and Mediterranean influences. The presentations were, in general, much less elaborate than in Nouvelle dishes. These developments were labeled in the press as *casual fine dining* and *Contemporary American "cuisine"* (Brenner 1999).

◎ FUSION STYLE

The idea of creating hybrids of French and another cuisine eventually led to what is called *Fusion*. Fusion style is yet another example of a name not precisely suited to what it is defining. As any serious student of culinary art knows, all cuisines are expanded and developed by fusing in new elements and concepts from other cuisines. Fusion in Professional cuisine was not just the inclusion of foods and flavors that had not been traditionally combined before, but an obvious, intentional juxtaposing of cuisines on the same plate or in the same menu. A simple example that works very well is Asian chicken salad; it fuses the concept of the American chicken salad with ingredients and flavors of Asia. Instead of dressing the salad with mayonnaise, the chicken might be dressed with a vinaigrette made from lemongrass oil, fish sauce, and sake. Peanuts, cilantro, and red Thai chilis might be used to replace the celery and onions of the more traditional version. Then, the salad might be presented on a bed of fried bean noodles or shredded cabbage, instead of in a sandwich or tomato cup.

Other examples of properly fused dishes are:

FIGURE 6.2

Asian-Influenced Chicken
Salad

◆ Shishito Pepper Rellenos   Mexican dish, Japanese ingredients
◆ Tuna Carpaccio with Habanero Salsa   Italian dish, Mexican ingredients
◆ Vegetable Tempura with Peppered   Japanese dish, Italian ingredients
    Pecorino Cheese

What makes a fused dish work is an invisible understanding on the chef's part of how an ingredient or technique functions in both the "original cuisine" and the "fused cuisine." These types of understandings will be discussed in greater depth in Chapter 10. For now, recognize that in each of the previous examples, the focus food holds meaning in both cuisines being fused: chicken is a widely used ingredient in both Asia and America, peppers are used in both Mexico and Japan, and fried foods are served in similar dishes in both Japan and Italy.

Chef Norman Van Aken is often referred to as the father of *New World cuisine*. Chef Van Aken, while working in Florida during the 1980s, fused influences from many diverse traditions including Floridian, Cuban, Caribbean, African, Latin, and Asian traditions to create contemporary translations. In an interview on *StarChefs.com*, he captures the heart of this type of culinary growth: "In my cooking, I create an interplay, a fusion, between regionalism and technical know-how" (Morse 2011).

Fusion within Professional cuisine has always been a way of growth. For example, Chefs Mary Sue Milliken and Susan Feniger opened CITY restaurant in Los Angeles in 1985; there, they blended influences from Thailand, India, and Mexico with skills acquired in fine French restaurants. That same year, the two chefs opened Border Grill in Santa Monica, an upscale Mexican restaurant.

So, regional and national cuisines never before seen in fine dining were making top reviews. Chef Rick Bayless, who had opened Frontera Grill in Chicago during 1987, developed Topolobampo, one of the nation's first fine-dining Mexican restaurants, next door in 1989. Thus, Fusion could also be the translation of a previously unrecognized cuisine to an upscale Euro-American format.

At times in this book I have noted a chef in relation to a style of Professional cuisine. This does not mean that the chef is still working in that style, or that other chefs who worked or are working in a similar way are less important. Many chefs go unrecognized throughout their career yet have a profound influence in the profession. The work of any chef is always evolving, and descriptions of their work might not fit their perception of what they are currently doing. Food writers often give labels to a chef's style that the chef would articulate differently; this is changing as chefs become more active participants in describing culinary styles. The references are provided as samples from a vast culinary panorama.

◎ THE MENU AND SERVICE

It was not so much that the menu structure or service style changed during the 1970s and 1980s, but rather, it was the expectations of the diner that changed. Diners wanted a more relaxed dining atmosphere, with menus and waiters that did not intimidate them. Artistic dining, up until this point, had been grounded in a relationship of expectations; diners were expected to know something about the classical repertoire and menu sequence. It was a type of connoisseurship, and chefs working in Nouvelle style played with this knowledge to create new experiences. Now, however, many people who could afford to experience artistic dining did not have a background in the Classical format. In response, kitchen and dining room staffs needed to adapt to create meaningful experiences for a new type of diner.

FIGURE 6.3

Ice Cream Cone–Styled Salmon Tartare. New meaning in dining is often created by elevating a dish that people have experienced many times by changing the ingredients or changing the presentation. This type of effect is epitomized by Chef Thomas Keller's iconic creation of *Salmon tartare with red onion crème fraiche in a savory tuile.*

There were still nine course menus in the most formal restaurants, and the five-course sequence was still very popular, but three-course menus were gaining in popularity. In some restaurants, the course sequences also began to be titled in more familiar language such as *starters* to replace the category of appetizers and *main course* to replace the category of entrées.

◆ Appetizer   →   Starter
◆ Entrée   →   Main course
◆ Dessert

> In a French menu, an *entrée* is a smaller course that precedes the main course. It would be an appetizer on an American menu.

The cheese and salad course was now often fused into a salad with cheese as an appetizer. The salad might even be found as a main course, as Spa "cuisine," with its emphasis on lightness, gained in popularity. It was also common to see duos and trios of items served in one course. For example, three small servings of different soups might be served as a soup sampler under the category of appetizers. Surf and Turf, a main course generally consisting of steak and lobster tail, became popular in America during the 1970s, and could be considered as a combination of the fish and main courses in a Classical menu.

The idea that a menu should begin with hot or cold disappeared. Even the concept of separating hot from cold foods on the same plate was changing as dishes such as steak salad became popular. Pasta and rice dishes were becoming main courses instead of side dishes. Comfort foods such as macaroni and cheese were being served in upscale versions using artisan cheeses and adding such ingredients as lobster.

The language used to write artistic dining menus changed during these styles from predominantly French to English. Instead of writing:

Côtelette de Porc aux pommes de terre croustillantes
Sauce Charcutière

on a New American style menu this might be written as:

Grilled Grengras Ranch Pork Chops with crispy Yukon Gold potatoes,
and a Riesling wine sauce finished with cornichons and onions

Of course, these changes in ingredients and course offerings, and new expressions of regional cuisines, led to new presentation designs on the plate.

PLATE DESIGN: ELEMENTAL

One of the earliest fusion hybrids was Franco-Japanese. While the flavors of this hybrid were still predominately western European, the look of the food was extrapolated from Japanese visual forms. Raw became a cooking method for European-based Professional cuisine. This style enlarged the idea of add-on garnishes using cut raw vegetables or edible leaves and flowers. The Japanese influence would also cause chefs to consider plates that were not round. This hybrid's visual plate representation can be generalized as *Elemental*.

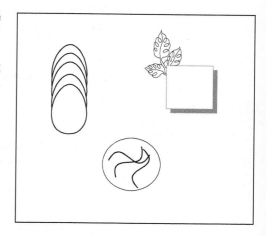

This is similar to the Face plate in that each flavor grouping is meant to be experienced separately from the others, but it goes further in the development of each element. Not only should each element relate to the other, but it should also function as complete on its own. It is almost a presentation of what could be separated into small dishes. In contrast to the Face plate dishes, which should be thought of as side dishes accompanying a focus food, the Elemental dishes should be thought of more as smaller, related appetizers. For example, an Elemental plate might consist of a small burrata drizzled with olive oil, a line of fried eggplant slices sprinkled with quinoa, and a square-cut portion of a tomato terrine.

New American style plates often combined more flavors into one course, and the fish course was often dropped from the menu. Instead, fish *or* meat could be the main course. Salad could be an opening course or, as developed in California "cuisine," a main course. Looking back to the beginning of Classical menus, we can see that not only were certain foods ordered before others, but culinary processes tended to be sequenced as well. New American style no longer follows this prescribed order of foods and culinary processes.

The division of certain foods into separate courses disappeared as hot and cold, meat and seafood, were sometimes served on the same plates. Many different plate designs emerged from this, including Duos / Trios, The Stack, The Mound, and BUFF.

PLATE DESIGN: DUOS / TRIOS

This plate design shows one focus food prepared in multiple ways. Through such designs, a chef can highlight the effects culinary processes have in producing different flavors of the same ingredient. Often in this design, small plates are used in conjunction with the large plate.

This would have never been done in the earlier plate designs, where plates never touched directly; for example, even soup bowls would have had a doily between the bowl and the supporting plate. This sort of plating created certain problems with eating utensils and sauce placement. The smaller plates required smaller spoons or forks than generally provided. Sauce used on foods presented directly on the larger plate often ran under the smaller plates, causing difficulty if the diner picked up these small dishes.

PLATE DESIGN: THE STACK

Chefs have always known that visual impact can be added by using the dimension of height. The concept of stacking is an expression of this knowledge, but it is unique because the best use of stacking creates a forced order of flavor appreciation. It is a wonderful example of how plate construction has now become one and the same with *dish* creation.

Nouvelle *dishes*, such as the stylized Tian, used stacking to elevate a rustic casserole into a plated construction, but stacking designs did not use a foundational *dish* as a concept. Rather, *dishes* were created by a visual desire to stack. We can see the Americaness of this concept in Blue Plate Specials of meatloaf piled on top of mashed potatoes and multilayered sandwich meals—a commingling of flavors and textures, temperatures, and courses. Elaborate stacking became a building process for some chefs, giving rise to plates that were called *architectural food*. Exaggerated height was the most important visual value of these dishes.

⊙ PLATE DESIGN: THE MOUND

Chefs have always used carefully chosen ingredients sourced from specialty producers, farms, or fisheries to denote value. Foods such as truffles, caviar, and foie gras belonged to an older category of exclusive luxury. While rarity and expense were still qualities of rank, provenance became the new status signifier. A studied casualness is expressed in the mound design. Chefs pile these special ingredients to create the appearance and flavor of a carefully constructed stew or sauté. Sauces are laced through the mound and lightly around it. These sauces often have textures that enable them to be dimensional, such as frothy emulsions. A tight mound may also be used as a pedestal with a focus food stacked against or on top of it, but then it is more of a Stack or BUFF design.

⊙ PLATE DESIGN: BUFF

The acronym of BUFF—balance, unity, focal point, flow—named the design that was formalized by chefs at the Culinary Institute of America. It is an effort to stylize *dishes* into a contemporary visual form.

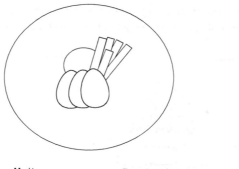

Balance   Unity   Focal point   Flow

Generally using the standard combination of meat, potato, and vegetable, these presentations unite foods in the center of the plate. The plate is visually divided into quadrants. The foods are then centered with an equal weight in each quadrant to provide balance. Flavor, color, shape, and texture choices are also balanced. Foods are arranged in strong lines that flow from the focused center. The focus food (protein) generally leans against a mounded starch with vegetables flowing out of the side (De Santis 1998).

> The bulleted list for Classical and Nouvelle styles were headed as tenets; from this
> point forward, the list is titled as guiding criteria. Fusion and subsequent styles
> are still being worked with, and tenets are too strict of a description for styles still
> evolving. Thus, they are described as guiding criteria.

GUIDING CRITERIA FOR
NEW AMERICAN / FUSION STYLES

- Contrast becomes the dominant value. Contrast in textures is emphasized. Contrast in temperatures is acceptable on a plate, if neither food is diminished by the exposure.

- Authentic flavors or cooking methods are translated to fit into plates or menus, emphasizing a hybrid cuisine.

- Juxtaposition of elements of different national or regional cuisines is valued. Plates and menus show a thematic harmony, demonstrated through the mastery of one cuisine with unexpected elements of others used as accents.

- Flavors may be very bold. Flavor counterpoints are used to emphasize differences, such as combining sweet with salty, or sour, or spicy, or smoky.

- Stack designs are used to create flavor. Foods should be stacked in a way that is easy to eat with the combined flavors best eaten in one forkful.

- Some height is valued in the design. Often, additional height may be achieved through the use of garnishes such as chips, tuiles, and fried items.

- Garnishes return as an add-on item. Flowers, uncooked cut vegetables, small greens, and leaves, as seen in Asian traditions, are used on hot foods.

- Emphasis is placed on the source of ingredients; which farm or artisan-producer supplied the foods is noted on menus.

- Bolder colored vegetables, such as purple potatoes or red peppers, are used to create vibrant contrast on the plate. Artificial or garish colors are avoided.

- Sauces based on bones and shells, to extend the flavor of the dominant protein, as well as sauces based on cream and butter, to extend richness, are used sparingly. Instead, highly spiced, sweet, or piquant sauces are used.

- Flavor themes may be presented throughout a menu, or in one course, by repeating ingredients in multiple dishes on a plate. Compartmentalized plates are also used to create this effect.

- The former principle of gently building up to stronger, heavier flavors as the meal progresses is not rigorously followed. This leads to menus that would sound like bold beats on a drum rather than a harmonizing chord leading to a crescendo.

- In longer menus, bolder flavors should not overwhelm the palate, causing following courses to be diminished. Rich, fatty flavors should not be used repeatedly in courses, and care should be given to their placement in the sequence so that the appetite is not deadened.

- Diversity of cuisines is embraced. Hierarchical categories of certain luxury foods versus everyday foods are disappearing.

QUERIES & INQUIRIES

1. What does it mean to have an eclectic style?
2. What is New American style? Who are some of the chefs associated with this style?
3. What is Fusion style? Who are some of the chefs associated with this style and what makes their work part of this style?
4. Although Fusion was a distinct style from New American in 1980s, is it still?
5. Were there changes to either menus or service for these styles?
6. What are the archetypal plate designs in Fusion / New American styles?
7. What are the guiding criteria of Fusion / New American styles?

8. Using the Classical dish that you had chosen for the inquiry in chapter 4, re-plate the ingredients and flavors to match the archetypal plate designs provided in this chapter. This can be done in the kitchen or through drawing. Write a menu description in the new style's language.

   If you have the opportunity to cook the *dish*, document your work with a photograph.

   a. What are your thoughts about the dish?
   b. Does this style of presentation express the desired flavors clearly?
   c. If you have cooked the dish, describe what eating it was like. Did the forms correspond to what you think of as food?
   d. Did the re-presentation of flavors change the taste of the dish? Was it an improvement?

CITATION AND REFERENCE MATERIALS

American Culinary Federation. "Who We Are." *American Culinary Federation*. 2008. Retrieved April 6, 2011, at www.acfchefs.org/Content/NavigationMenu2/About/Overview/default.htm.

Anderson, Jean. *The American Century Cookbook*. New York: Clarkson Potter Publishers, 1997.

Brenner, Leslie. *American Appetite*. New York: HarperCollins Publishers, Inc., 1999. p. 150.

"Chefs Susan Feniger and Mary Sue Milliken's Biography." *StarChefs.com*. 1998. Retrieved April 6, 2011, at www.starchefs.com/Tamales/bio.html.

The Culinary Institute of America. "The Story of the World's Premier Culinary College—A History of Excellence, Professional Advancement, and Innovation. *Culinary Institute of America*. 2011. Retrieved April 6, 2011, at www.cia chef.edu/about/history.asp.

De Santis, Ronald. "B.U.F.F.-Up on Food Presentation." *The National Culinary Review* (Feb. 1998): 6–10.

Dornenburg and Page, Karen. *Culinary Artistry*. New York: Van Nostrand Reinhold, 1996.

Dornenburg, Andrew, and Karen Page. *The New American Chef*. Hoboken, NJ: John Wiley & Sons, 2003.

Forgione, Larry. *An American Place*. New York: William Morrow and Company, Inc., 1996.

Keller, Thomas. *The French Laundry Cookbook*. New York: Artisan, 1999.

Keogh, Keith, and Culinary Team USA. *New Currents in American Cuisine*. Illinois: Cahners Publishing Company, 1993.

Keogh, Keith. "The Art of Plate Presentation." *The National Culinary Review*, (Sept. 1999): 30–34.

Langan, Marianne. "Accent on Garnishes." *The National Culinary Review* (May 1999): 13–16. Print.

Lovegren, Sylvia. *Fashionable Food: 7 Decades of Food Fads*. New York: MacMillan, 1995.

Morse, Jocelyn. "Norman Van Aken." *Interview on StarChefs .com*. n.d. Retrieved April 6, 2011, at www.starchefs.com/NVanAken/html/interview.shtml.

Page, Karen, and Dornenburg. *The Flavor Bible*. New York: Little, Brown and Company, 2008.

"Rick Bayless Biography." *StarChefs.com*. 1995–2009. Retrieved April 6, 2011, at www.starchefs.com/chefs/RBayless/html/biography.shtml.

Ridge, Diane, and Sarah Minasian. "Plate like the Pros." *Food Management* (May 1, 1999): n.p. Retrieved January 5, 2010, at foodmanagement.com/business_topics/menu_cuisine/plate-like-pros-0599/index.html.

Ruhlman, Michael. *The Reach of a Chef: Beyond the Kitchen.* New York, Viking Press, 2006.

Stechl, Hans-Albert, and Chris Meier. *The Culinary Chronicle.* Design. Hausch, Bruno. Ed. Hausch Messer, Christine. Trans. Spinner, Claudia. Bergdorf: Opt Art Lizenz AG, 1999.

Zagat guide. "Overview in About Us." *Zagat Survey.* 1999–2011. Retrieved April 6, 2011, at www.zagat.com/about-us.

CHAPTER 7

Plate Frame:
Global Style

Beginning around the mid-1990s, a new style of Professional cuisine was developing that reflected both a chef's personal viewpoint and a global style of expressing such a viewpoint shared across the professional world. Yet, New American styles and Fusion styles did not become less important. Instead, culinary art had reached an age of pluralism. There was no longer only one accepted concept of artistic dining, and there was no longer one dominant style of presentations.

In 1991, the **W**orld **W**ide **W**eb was launched, and in 1993, the Food Network first aired on television. The amount and diffusion of information about food and cooking had never been done so easily or so quickly. Images of food and ingredients from all over the world were only a click away. At the same time, chefs were becoming more than master cooks with a vision. They were becoming corporate business entities. An acclaimed chef might run multiple restaurants not only in the same country but across the world; so, such chefs influenced the development of cooks in their own kitchens as well as cooks looking at their work through these rapidly growing sources of information.

No longer characterized by elements from various ethnic cuisines juxtaposed on a plate, *Global style* uses ingredients, cooking techniques, and flavors from the worldwide market, all of which are blended to create *dishes* through plating in professional kitchens. Chefs were actively seeking new understandings across kitchens and traditions. They were communicating more openly with each other and they were more self-aware. Developments spread through cookbooks, the Internet, and other media, allowing a rapid dissemination

FIGURE 7.1

Grilled Watermelon Steak,
Baby Arugula, Lime,
Corn Syrup

of ideas to be responded to without concern for location. This was not a call for "anything goes," but rather, the creation of a dialogue of self- and community-knowledge.

Additionally, consumers in the 1990s became more concerned about and aware of ingredients in their food. The new Nutrition Labeling and Education Act required that health claims on food packages be backed up by labeling that met FDA standards. Consumers also became more concerned with how their food was grown and transported. Farmers' markets were established in cities across the country and organics became one of the fastest-growing sectors in the food industry. Diners no longer saw Fusion as new and accepted a wide variety of ingredients, like arugula and lemongrass, as standard fare. As a case in point, salsa was outselling ketchup in grocery stores.

As in other Professional styles, ingredients were the focus of Global style chefs, but the difference was the new way of seeing them. Ingredients were now seen as composites of characteristics, such as multiple flavor notes, colors, or micro-shapes. Plate presentations were often abstract compositions of ingredients' elements. Like Abstract artists, Global style chefs sought alternative ways of presenting flavor that reflected personalized understandings of a culinary world.

In the 1950s, American artists had changed the way the Art world thought about the United States. Abstract Expressionism, such as can be seen in the work of Jackson Pollack, helped make this shift possible. Long considered a secondary player compared to Europe, America came to be recognized as a world Art center. In the 1990s, American chefs brought this same type of recognition to U.S. dining.

American chefs created flavor pairings, dishes, and menu sequences that reflected a unique view of Professional cuisine. The success of Global style has led to an increased self-awareness of the creative process by all chefs, who, now more than ever, are more articulate about their personalized visions.

◎ GLOBAL STYLE

The creative process of Global style focuses on individual characteristics of ingredients, then chooses certain elements to highlight through texture or presentation changes. For example, a cauliflower floret is made up of many tiny florets tightly packed together; by separating these micro-florets on the plate the idea of cauliflower is abstracted into a scatter pattern. Working in this more abstract way is the most difficult of presentation designs

FIGURE 7.2

A Fish Course. In this Global style presentation, the many flavors in the dish have been given a new texture. There are foams, powders, and oils. Can you recognize Fried Catfish with Tartar Sauce?

because without a previous understanding of Professional cuisine, such abstractions can lack depth of flavor and cohesiveness.

Ironically, while the source of ingredients is increasingly important, and free-range and organic are standard listings in menus, chefs simultaneously have begun exploring ingredients used in industrial food processing. Different starches and gelling agents are experimented with to create new textures. One of the first to be worked with was foams, which are often created in canisters charged with nitrous oxide. Gelatin, not used extensively since Classical preparations, has become popular again. Cubes and even sheets of gelled flavors are used on plates. This increased interest in a more scientific method of food preparation has continued into the twenty-first century.

In other styles, sauces are generally used to deepen or contrast the focus food, relating back to the method used to cook them. Global style often does not have a single focus food but rather many foci on a plate. Thus, without a dominant focus food, each ingredient is considered separately for cooking method or process, resulting in sauces that are more independent and that become a more separate element on the plate.

The range of sauces had already expanded from the original six mothers during Nouvelle, New American, and Fusion styles. In Global style, sauce-making methods proliferated. Chef Jean-George Vongerichten, author of *Simple Cuisine*, was an early leader in such methods, with his "building blocks" of juices, vinaigrettes, flavored oils, and broths. Chef Charlie Trotter increased awareness of such new sauce types in his cookbooks, using "waters," syrups, and frothy emulsions in his dishes (Vongerichten 1990; Trotter 1996).

FIGURE 7.3

Another Global Style Fish Course. In this presentation, salmon is served with an accompanying sauce. Imagine eating this visually attractive presentation; there would not be enough sauce to go with every bite of salmon.

These newer-style sauces, in turn, gave rise to multiple placement methods. Instead of covering foods, or covering the plate, sauces are minimized to puddles, dots, smears, and brushes. In some instances, the design element of the sauce becomes more important to the look of the plate than the flavor; there is not always a correlation between sauce amount and food bites. Powdered ingredients are scattered or formed into lines instead of mixed into *dishes*, creating the idea of dry condiments.

The experimentation of new flavor associations in Global style made space for the blurring of lines between the sweet and savory courses. Course flavors traditionally associated with savory plates, such as vegetables, herbs, and pepper, are used in desserts and vice versa. For example, vanilla is subtly used with poached shrimp, or chilies are paired with chocolate. This is reminiscent of flavor combinations in the earlier Room Frame *dishes*.

FIGURE 7.4

Amuse-bouche

◎ THE MENU AND SERVICE

The courses of menus in previous styles provided the diner with choices between different dishes. In Global style, it is more often the case that the chef will decide on the dish to be served in each course and the diner chooses between complete menus. This type of Global menu is referred to as a *tasting menu*. Another style of menu often used in Global style is a *small plate menu,* also sometimes referred to as a snack menu or sharing menu. These menus offer dishes in different groupings that allow the diners to create their own menu sequence and are often ordered for the table, allowing the diners to share.

Menu sequences had previously opened with canapés or hors d'oeuvre, but in Global style, the diner begins with an *amuse-bouche*. Literally meaning, "mouth amuser," these tiny bites are offered just after the diner orders, at the discretion of the chef—they are not part of the order. Amuse-bouches are often served on an eating utensil, such as a spoon. The customer would take the spoon off a service-plate held by the server and eat the spoonful directly.

The idea of side dishes accompanying the focus food disappears in Global style; instead, the plate design unites flavors to create a *dish*. This can be seen in the menu descriptions of foods that read like a list of ingredients. Without a focus food, the sequence of the menu courses changed. Global style menus often use either a small plate format, where diners choose multiple dishes without concern for sequence, or a tasting menu of "small bites" sequenced by the chef.

An Example of a Sampling from a Small Plates Menu

COLD
acorn prosciutto
nopales' tuna tartare, pine nuts
pickled candle corn, micro greens salad

WARM
mission olives
wild turkey confit, grilled crostini
wood-oven baked bread, two butters

HOT
grilled poblano peppers, goat cheese
blue crab croquettes, sweet chili remoulade
wagyu (American kobe beef) skewers

SWEET
Szechwan pepper-dusted doughnut holes
vanilla roasted pineapple
smoked chocolate pudding

An Example of a Tasting Menu

Melon Caviar—Sturgeon Cheeks

Roasted Radish Foam, Pumpernickel Sea-Salt Tuile, Pea Shoots

Seared Sea Urchin Tongues, Pickled Violet Artichokes, Micro-Shiso

Mi-cuit Mackerel, Buckwheat Risotto, Cucumber Butter

Noble Sour Sorbet

64-minute Brown Egg—Sautéed Agretti

Clay Roasted Chicken, Round Carrots, Black Corn

Cherry-Smoked Bacon, Braised Oxtail, Celery Root Puree

Absinthe Granité

Peppered Foie Gras—Peach Jelly

Crushed Strawberries, Saffron Cream, Green Walnuts

Criollo Chocolate Cake—Madagascar Vanilla Sauce

Elemental and Duos / Trios plate designs within New American / Fusion styles had begun the conceptualization of small, sample offerings within a course. In Global, these types of offerings are separated out into individual *dishes*. Mezze (Middle Eastern), zakuski (Russian), dim sum (Chinese), tapas (Spanish), and hors d'oeuvre (French) are all types of small foods that are served in specific settings in their traditional origins. This type of food was not conventionally considered a main meal but rather as dishes that would stimulate the appetite; or, as dishes to be eaten in a period between meals or while waiting for a meal. In contrast, small plate menus use these types of dishes to allow a diner to create a meal. They may be listed by principle ingredient under headings such as beef or vegetable, or they may be listed by temperature under headings such as hot and cold. The diners usually order for the table, creating a personalized miniature buffet.

In Global style, the chef's tasting menu, or menu degustation, is paramount. Chefs had long before offered tasting menus embedded in an à la carte menu. So, if an à la carte menu had the course sequence of appetizer, fish course, meat course, salad, cheese, and dessert, so too would the chef's tasting menu. But in Global style, the chef's tasting menu often differs from the à la carte courses offered—there are more courses that do not fit any one course listed. Rather, they are smaller, often consisting of one to three bites, and separated into larger sequences of 12 to 24 courses.

Often, separate course offerings are not listed—instead, there are two tasting menus offered, one of around 12 courses and the other of about 24 courses. The diner, in choosing either, gives control over to the chef to decide what and in what order dishes will be eaten. Such menus might be themed around a season or a flavor. Individual courses are also sometimes themed to express one flavor in multiple ways. Elements of styles and designs from all previous periods could be reflected in these minimized courses without consistency from course to course. In short, sequencing certain foods and culinary processes in a prescribed order has become ambiguous.

The language used in Global menus reflects the changing ideas of course headings. Menu offerings might now be grouped because of like ingredients, temperature, cooking method, or even, degrees of doneness. The items listed under the headings are written primarily based on ingredients or flavors.

So the menu item from the last chapter, written as:

Grilled Grengras Ranch Pork Chops with crispy Yukon Gold potatoes, and a Riesling wine sauce finished with cornichons and onions

On a Global menu this dish might be written as:

grilled pork chop, crispy potatoes, soft onions, pickles, mustard emulsion

Global serviceware includes not only plates of various shapes—circles, rectangles, and triangles—but also of different materials, such as glass or stone. Manufacturers have responded by creating lines with pieces such as bowl-plates, large-rimmed plates with centered cup depressions, elongated ovals that taper and balloon out, and compartmentalized asymmetrical shapes. As such, there is a new emphasis on the serving vessel as part of the presentation. Now, not only is plating used to make a *dish* but also the very "dish" itself serves as part of the creation.

FIGURE 7.5

A Plate Assortment. This image shows examples of the different plate shapes available to the contemporary chef.

◎ PLATE DESIGN: LINEAR

These presentations on variously shaped serviceware use long and narrow slices of proteins and vegetables. The sauce is stretched into elongated dots or smears. A brush is sometimes used to lay down sauce, creating a textured background.

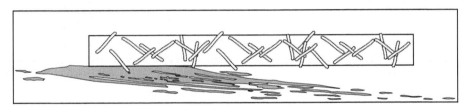

◎ PLATE DESIGN: COURSE WITHIN A COURSE

Expanding on the Elemental and Duos / Trios plate presentations, chefs began to sequence the order of dishes within plates, directing the diner in which order the plate should best be eaten. One course now sequences flavors in a miniature version of a themed menu. Each dish provides a flavor that is one step away from the other on the plate, like courses within a course.

This combination of hot and cold dishes within one course is conceptually different from earlier styles. Previously, add-on garnishes of cold ingredients, such as fruit segments, tender herbs, or flowers had been used on some hot plates. Nouvelle and New American style salads might have been topped with hot ingredients, such as cheese or meat. Global style furthers the contrast by using hot layers on cold layers, as well as cold dishes and hot dishes on the same plate. For example, a carrot sorbet might top hot minted peas, or the mini-plates might progress from a cold squid seviche to a hot squid ink risotto. The rules about serving temperatures of foods have become clouded. It is not possible to follow the tenet that hot foods are served hot and cold foods are served cold on correspondingly warmed or chilled plates, for these newer dishes were neither one nor the other.

PLATE DESIGN: DECONSTRUCTION / ABSTRACTION

Since the late 1990s, ingredients have been separated out of a *dish* to isolate flavors. New textures are sometimes given to the ingredients; then, these ingredients are reunited in an abstract plate presentation, which fragments the appearance. There is no longer one focal point, but many competing foci. The food elements may be related to each other, so that when eaten, the plate culminates in a flavor reminiscent of a traditional *dish*, or they may create a new *dish* that highlights the disparate elements. The look

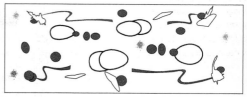

of these plates can be like small hors d'oeuvre connected by drizzles and dots of sauce.

GUIDING CRITERIA FOR GLOBAL STYLE

As in the last chapter on New American and Fusion style, this style is reviewed with guiding criteria rather than major tenets. An interesting development in Global style is that it is now more often chefs who articulate their style than interpreters outside of the kitchen.

◆ Global style is concept driven. Thus, chefs need to think about expressing food ideas. A maturity of professional experience is necessary for this type of conceptualization to work.

◆ Tasting menus are the best way to experience these designs. The customer should not choose the sequence of foods.

◆ Conversely, a small plate menu format allows the customer to have complete control of sequencing foods.

◆ Small bites are best. Each course of a menu should be one to three mouthfuls.

◆ The menu is written to highlight the ingredients used. Finding new and different ingredients that are part of an unknown market is inspiring.

◆ The hierarchy of sequencing foods has become less rigorous. Cold is no longer separated into separate courses.

◆ Cold can be contrasted with warmer temperatures on the same plate.

◆ The use of many different textures on one plate is crucial.

◆ The physical attributes of ingredients are the starting point of creativity. The primary tastes of the ingredients are extrapolated into new forms and textures.

◆ Cooking processes are used to create abstract textures. Previously, the characteristics of the foods suggested cooking method, such as tougher muscle need to be braised; now, how to achieve a new texture guides cooking processes.

◆ Any food may be a focus food, not only animal proteins.

◆ There are no luxury foods, such as truffles or foie gras; instead, all foods may be elevated in importance through design.

◆ Bone-based stocks are not that important, especially fish stock. Sauces not based in traditional hearth or Professional cuisines have been created.

◆ Smears, valleys, mohawks, brushes, sheets, and cubes are seen as new ways of plating sauces.

◆ The serviceware changes from flat, round plateware to shapes that suggest new placements of ingredients.

◆ Chefs working in this style lead up to the next menu type: a service style and menu that is no longer bound by the plate but by an interactive table setting.

QUERIES & INQUIRIES

1. What is Global style? Who are some of the chefs associated with this style?

2. Were there changes to either menus or service for this style?

3. What makes Global style different from Fusion style?

4. What are the archetypal plate designs in Global style?

5. Surf and Turf was mentioned in the last chapter as a main course that combined the earlier, separate fish and meat courses. Which design do you think best represents this plate: Fusion's Elemental design or Global's Course within a Course design?

6. What are the guiding criteria of Global style?

7. Using the Classical dish that you had chosen for the inquiry in Chapter 4, re-plate the ingredients and flavors to match the archetypal plate designs provided in this chapter. This can be done in the kitchen or through drawing. Write a menu description in the new style's language.

   If you have the opportunity to cook the *dish,* document your work with a photograph.

   a. What are your thoughts about the *dish*?
   b. Does this style of presentation express the desired flavors clearly?
   c. If you have cooked the *dish*, describe what eating it was like. Did the forms correspond to what you think of as food?
   d. Did the re-presentation of flavors change the taste of the dish? Was it an improvement?

QUERIES & INQUIRIES *Continued*

8. Chapters 4–7 outlined the archetypal plate designs in artistic dining. At the very beginning of the book, in the prologue, you were asked to create a plate by drawing a design onto one of the two plate outlines. Look back at what you created.

   a. Does it resemble any of the designs in Chapters 4–7?

      If it does, do you think that the style it is associated with matches yours?
      If it does not, what do you think distinguishes your design? Were you working in a different food category, price point, service style, or menu format?

   b. Knowing what you do after working this far in the book, would you do your original plate design differently?

CITATION AND REFERENCE MATERIALS

Anderson, Jean. *The American Century Cookbook*. New York: Clarkson Potter Publishers, 1997.

Bundy, Beverly. *The Century in Food*. Oregon: Collection Press, Inc., 2002.

Mennell, Stephen. *All Manners of Food*. 2nd ed. Chicago: University of Illinois Press, 1996.

Ruhlman, Michael. *The Reach of a Chef: Beyond the Kitchen*. New York, Viking Press, 2006.

Phaidon Press, editors. *Coco: 10 World-leading Masters Choose 100 Contemporary Chefs*. London: Phaidon Press Limited, 2009.

Trotter, Charlie. *Charlie Trotter's Vegetables*. California: Ten Speed Press, 1996.

"The United States and Canada, 1900 A.D.–present." In Heilbrunn Timeline of Art History. New York: The Metropolitan Museum of Art, 2000–(October 2004). Retrieved April 7, 2011, at www.metmuseum.org/toah/ht/?period=11&ion=na.

Vongerichten, Jean-George. *Simple Cuisine*. New York: Prentice Hall, 1990.

The Emerging Menu:
Interactive Table Setting

 BACKGROUND

Chapter 3 presented three different *Frames* for the *culinary Art history*: the Room, the Table, and the Plate. These Frames are analogous to periods in Art history; the difference is that the Frames are not as linear and that the Frames are not defined by time periods. Rather, culinary Frames are defined by the course structure of menus and the style of service used. The possibility that a new Frame is developing, therefore, has to be considered in terms of changes to menu course structure and service style.

Beginning after 2000, new ideas started to be discussed in the food world centering around the concept *molecular gastronomy*. The phrase developed out of a 1992 workshop organized by Cooking Instructor Elizabeth Cawdy Thomas, Professor Nicholas Kurti, and Author Harold McGee, originally held under the name "Science and Gastronomy" and later titled "Molecular and Physical Gastronomy." After the first, McGee was no longer an organizer but participated in all five subsequent seminars. The workshops focused on traditional culinary preparations and how a scientific understanding of cooking would be beneficial. In 1999, after Professor Kutri died, Hervè This, who also assisted in the planning of these workshops, retitled the next meeting "International Workshop on Molecular Gastronomy 'N. Kutri.'" Professor This has continued to develop this field (McGee 2008).

The catch phrase *molecular gastronomy* took on a life of its own. Chefs disavowed being molecular gastronomists, food writers continued to define chefs and restaurants with the phrase, and thus confusion grew. Is it a style of cooking or a scientific method of investigating food and cooking? Science is a methodology to produce knowledge; technology is a means of applying that knowledge; Art is an expression of creativity that provokes an emotional response; and cooking is all of these concepts—it is a craft. A craft methodology uses an older sense of production before specialization. So chefs who use scientific understandings in their cooking, no matter how new the under-standings are or how new the technologies are that are used to apply these new understanding in food production, are still craft based. They are weaving together knowledge from science, tech-nology, and art through manual production; thus, chefs are not molecular gastronomists. Craft work in the modern world is collaboration between specialists.

So if molecular gastronomy is a scientific field, what should the chefs working with and helping develop this knowledge as it is applied to food creations be called? The style of such chefs has been labeled as techno-emotive, avant-garde, and alchemic. Of the three labels listed, I would suggest that Techno-emotive is best; it weaves together art and technology. Avant-garde will become obsolete once something new comes along; and while alchemy is about transforming substances, it predates modern chemistry, which is very important in this style.

The question, then, is if Techno-emotive style is part of the Plate Frame or a new frame. If it is indeed a new frame and not part of the Global style, then it might stand as postmodern does to modern in Art history. There is certainly not a consensus that postmodern is something separate from the modern period in the arts. While modernism is generally associated with a rejection of tradition and certainty, it still participates in continuity and contextual meaning. By contrast, postmodernism rejects the idea of continuity and fragments contextual meaning. Thus, postmodern art does not represent a continuation of work, but rather a deconstruction of the system of past works.

Modern art was originally called avant-garde art in the beginning of the twentieth century; postmodern art would not be considered the edge moving forward but a break with the story of Art. Postmodern art has a sense of irony; it is a recycling of art through decon-struction understood by fragmented subcultures (Irvine 2007).

Certainly Techno-emotive style has elements that are associated with postmodern art, such as its sense of playfulness, deconstruction, and reassembly of past works, and the mixing of popular with elite forms; but, the chefs exploring this style continually affirm a continuity with Professional cuisine. Thus, in terms of the comparison of Techno-emotive style to postmodern art, Techno-emotive style would still be a modern movement instead of a postmodern movement.

Deciding if Techno-emotive style is the first style in the beginning of a new frame instead of being the latest within the Plate Frame requires examination of any changes in the menu structure and service style. But, any conclusive answer cannot be determined, as it is too much of the present to be able to have any reasonable perspective.

FIGURE 8.1

Mussels and Beer.
The pipette in this picture is set to serve mussels with an accompanying broth. Traditionally, pipettes are used in scientific laborato-ries to transfer liquids.

⊙ TECHNO-EMOTIVE STYLE

Inspiration for *dishes* and plate constructions previously centered on hearth-based cuisines, other work in professional cuisine, and/or food elements from diverse markets. In this emerging menu frame, creation came not only from these three areas, but more importantly, from food science. Using scientific knowledge about how tastes are experienced and experimenting with food processing technologies, Techno-emotive chefs created courses that engaged the senses through alternative conveyances.

Culinary creation has always advanced through the application of new technologies. Ice cream was revolutionary when it was first made because flavors previously only associated with fruits or vegetables were made into ice crystals. Gelatin has long been used to give different shapes to flavors; air has been trapped in whipped flavors to create different textures. Currently, with the ability to separate isolated flavor molecules, new foods and flavors can be created; this design method is called *culinary constructionism*.

Chef Ferran Adrià is considered the premier chef of what is often referred to as Techno-emotive style. Adrià and his team created a workshop/lab, elBullitaller, where, during months when elBulli restaurant was closed, the scientific method was applied to food creation. The results have helped to define this style's philosophy and have created influential concepts and techniques. A 23-point synthesis of elBulli cuisine has been posted on its website.

The 23rd point states, "Knowledge and/or collaboration with experts from different fields (gastronomic culture, history, industrial design, etc.) is essential for progress in cooking. In particular collaboration with the food industry and the scientific world has brought about fundamental advances" (Elbulli.com n.d.).

Essential collaboration can be seen in the work of Chef Pierre Gagnaire and Professor Hervè This. *"Constructivisme culinaire"* is the result of the application of such scientific findings by Chef Gagnaire. *"Il ne s'agit pas de déconstruire, mais de construire!"* (Gagnaire 2010). "It is not about deconstruction, but construction!" (author's translation).

The difference between the deconstruction of Global and the construction of Techno-emotive is key. Professor This explains it in terms of music. Previously, chefs always played chords of flavors; for example, a carrot is a chord. Techno-emotive chefs play notes of flavor; sucrose

FIGURE 8.2

Spherification. By dropping flavorful liquid mixed with a gelling agent into a specialized bath, spheres are formed. These can be made in various sizes, from "caviar" to "yolk."

is one note found in carrots. By knowing the various compounds found in foods, which together create their flavor chord, the notes (chemical compounds) can be isolated and constructed into new flavors. "Culinary Constructivism prefers artificial rather than natural" (This 2007).

The goal is for diners to experience an emotion instead of traditional flavors. Professor This and Chef Adrià have both created symbol systems to express their work in food— a nomenclature of symbols to replace the narrative recipe. Hot gelatins, dry frozen pow-

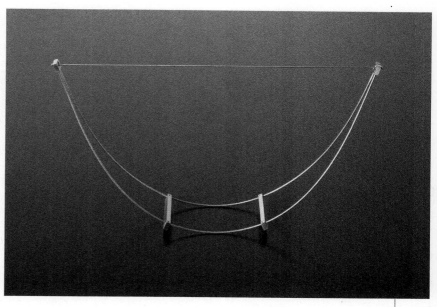

FIGURE 8.3

The Bow. This piece of creative serviceware is called the "bow;" it allows food to be served suspended. Chef Grant Achatz collaborated with Martin Kastner of Crucial Detail to design such innovative serviceware to serve foods in new ways.

ders, hot liquids suspended or layered on cold liquids, spheres of liquid, spirals of solid oil, and vegetable airs are all used to elevate basic flavors to surprise and enchant diners.

◎ MENU AND SERVICE: INTERACTIVE TABLE SETTING

Correspondingly, the presentation of these textures (*dishes*) as complete courses, or focus food, has greatly changed service. This parallels the impact that performance art has had on the general perception of what Art is. For example, service personnel now need to direct the diner in how to best interact with these new presentations. Diners may be directed not to mix the elements in a bowl, or to eat from one end of the plate to the other, or to drink a small glass or eat a bite in one mouthful. To achieve these results Chef Achatz, of Alinea restaurant in Chicago, collaborates with a designer, Martin Kastner of Crucial Detail, to create nontraditional serviceware. The end performance results in the desired art of the presentation (chefg 2004).

Previously in Plate menus, a chef's tasting menu (*dégustation*) would be extrapolated out of course structures already existing in the à la carte offerings. The tasting offered by Techno-emotive chefs is the menu; generally, no à la carte service is available. The menus do not follow a formalized course sequence. The question of how these smaller dishes are sequenced is still being worked out. When presenting a series of hors d'œuvre like dishes, does the meat come in the middle of the menu? Do flavors build in intensity? Are temperatures grouped in the sequence cold follows hot or hot leads to cold? Is there a priority of textures or cooking methods? Are courses grouped by eating methods?

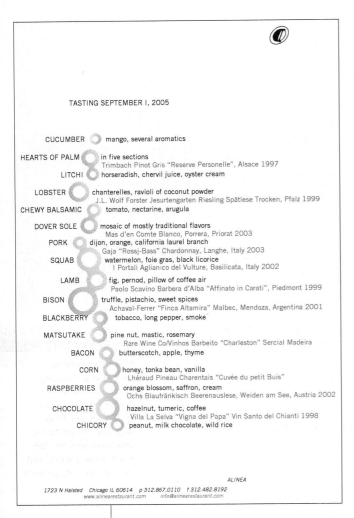

TASTING SEPTEMBER I, 2005

CUCUMBER		mango, several aromatics
HEARTS OF PALM		in five sections
		Trimbach Pinot Gris "Reserve Personelle", Alsace 1997
LITCHI		horseradish, chervil juice, oyster cream
LOBSTER		chanterelles, ravioli of coconut powder
		J.L. Wolf Forster Jesurtengarten Riesling Spätlese Trocken, Pfalz 1999
CHEWY BALSAMIC		tomato, nectarine, arugula
DOVER SOLE		mosaic of mostly traditional flavors
		Mas d'en Comte Blanco, Porrera, Priorat 2003
PORK		dijon, orange, california laurel branch
		Gaja "Rossj-Bass" Chardonnay, Langhe, Italy 2003
SQUAB		watermelon, foie gras, black licorice
		I Portali Aglianico del Vulture, Basilicata, Italy 2002
LAMB		fig, pernod, pillow of coffee air
		Paolo Scavino Barbera d'Alba "Affinato in Carati", Piedmont 1999
BISON		truffle, pistachio, sweet spices
		Achaval-Ferrer "Finca Altamira" Malbec, Mendoza, Argentina 2001
BLACKBERRY		tobacco, long pepper, smoke
MATSUTAKE		pine nut, mastic, rosemary
		Rare Wine Co/Vinhos Barbeito "Charleston" Sercial Madeira
BACON		butterscotch, apple, thyme
CORN		honey, tonka bean, vanilla
		Lhéraud Pineau Charentais "Cuvée du petit Buis"
RASPBERRIES		orange blossom, saffron, cream
		Ochs Blaufränkisch Beerenauslese, Weiden am See, Austria 2002
CHOCOLATE		hazelnut, tumeric, coffee
		Villa La Selva "Vigna del Papa" Vin Santo del Chianti 1998
CHICORY		peanut, milk chocolate, wild rice

ALINEA

1723 N Halsted　Chicago IL 60614　p 312.867.0110　f 312.482.8192
www.alinearestaurant.com　info@alinearestaurant.com

FIGURE 8.4

Alinea menu.

Courtesy of Chef Grant Achatz.

The answers to such questions are being created in contemporary practice; for example, Chef Achatz works on the idea of sequencing by denoting the intensity or size of his courses on the printed menu with circles of various placements and size. Chef Adrià, on ElBulli menus, seemed to group eating methods; items eaten without a fork or items eaten with a spoon were coupled with themes of flavors. Menus might also be arranged based on culinary processes used to create the various courses. Techno-emotive menus end with savory becoming slightly sweet, followed by sweet being slightly savory, ascending to the sweetest dishes (Alinea 2005; Adrià, Adrià, and Soler 2003).

Flavors are considered as elements that could be separated not only from traditional pairing, but from foods themselves. These flavors can then be expressed through a variety of textures not normally associated with the original flavor. These type of flavor creations began in Global style; remember the deconstructed Catfish and Tartar Sauce on page 69? The flavors of tartar sauce were separated into ingredients, which were then given new textures. Powdered oil, lemon juice, capers and egg yolks mounded next to frozen pickle relish were abstractly presented with the catfish so that when the diner moved through the plate, the combined effects of each ingredient would synergize into the traditional flavor of tartar sauce. In this potentially new frame, the flavors might be even further enhanced using scented air or dissolving tablets to remind the diner of a traditional fish fry. This moves the experience off the plate, somewhat out of the mouth, into the mind of a diner.

The language of the menus has also changed to emphasize flavors rather than ingredients. Meat is no longer the center stage; vegetables, fruits, and nuts are highlighted. The idea of luxury food items has disappeared. "All products have the same gastronomic value, regardless of their price." The idea of garnishing is once again inherent in the food itself; add-ons are not necessary. Point 14 states that, ". . . in main dishes the product-garnish-sauce hierarchy is being broken down" (elBulli.com n.d.: points 3, 4, 14 of synthesis).

A BACKWARD GLANCE

Techno-emotive chefs' culinary constructionism, change of food values and meal sequences, and change in service style suggest the possibility of a new menu frame. Yet chefs using constructionism often refer back to a previous style through deconstruction or irony. In this style, not only are dishes deconstructed and reassembled but the elements of individual foods are deconstructed and reformed into new food products. Food is re-presented as a thoughtful concept. The uses of unexpected elements create emotions, not only through performance but also through the use of provocative textures and temperatures, achieved through food processing technologies.

Chefs are now working both forward and backward among design influences. The emerging menu and service style bear similarities in flavor affinities, emotional responses of diners, and the importance of service personnel to Room menus of the Medieval and Renaissance periods. Chefs working in these earlier periods might shape foie gras to look like swans, or place live birds within a pie crust, so that when experienced by the diner, emotions of surprise and delight are triggered by the unfamiliar expressed in the familiar. Techno-emotive chefs also aspire to play on diners' emotions using the unfamiliar to suggest the familiar. The idea of a menu ending with the sweetest dish has been in practice since the end of the Room menus, but the line is once again being blurred. Ironically, even the look of foods from these two periods might share similarities. One striking example is Ferran Adrià's hot jellied consommé with veal marrow from the elBulli 1998–2002 cookbook and Ivan Day's historic recreation of a rosewater-flavored jelly served at Henry VIII's garter feast given at Windsor in 1520 (Adrià, Adrià, and Soler 2003, 37; Day n.d., jelly).

FIGURE 8.5

A New Blancmange. An example, following the presentations of Chef Adrià's Hot Jellied Consommé and Chef Ivan Day's re-creation of Rosewater-flavored Jelly, using jellied almond milk and saffron chicken broth.

QUERIES & INQUIRIES

1. What does the phrase *molecular gastronomy* mean?

2. What is Techno-emotive style? Who are some of the chefs associated with this style?

3. Were there changes to either menus or service for this style?

4. Do you think that Techno-emotive style is part of the Plate Frame or that it is the first style in a new Frame?

5. Use the Classical dish that you had chosen for the inquiry in Chapter 4 and re-plate the ingredients and flavors to match the archetypal plate designs provided in this chapter. This can be done in the kitchen or through drawing. Write a menu description in the new style's language.

If you have the opportunity to cook the *dish,* document your work with a photograph.

a. What are your thoughts about the dish?

b. Does this style of presentation express the desired flavors clearly?

c. If you have cooked the *dish,* describe what eating it was like. Did the forms of the dishes correspond to what you think of as food?

d. Did the re-presentation of flavors change the taste of the dish? Was it an improvement?

CITATION AND REFERENCE MATERIALS

Adrià, Ferran, Albert Adrià, and Juli Soler. *elBulli 1998–2002.* Spain: Impresiones Generales S.A., 2003.

chefg [Achatz, Grant.]. "Alinea Serviceware a collaboration with Crucial Detail." *eG Forums.* Posted Aug. 23, 2004. Copyright © 2001–2009 by the eGullet Society for Culinary Arts & Letters. Retrieved January 7, 2011, at forums.egullet.org/index.php?showtopic=49816.

Day, Ivan. "Jelly, Flummery and Creams." *historicfood.com.* Galleries tab: Historic Food Mould Links: Jelly Moulds—General Information. n.d. Retrieved January 8, 2010, at www.historic food.com/Jellies.htm.

ElBulli. "Synthesis of elBulli Cuisine." Elbulli.com. elBulli, n.d. Retrieved January 7, 2010, at www.elbulli.com/videos/sintesis/preindex.php?lang=en.

Gagnaire, Pierre, and Hervè This. "Notre idée" Art and Science. *pierregagnaire.com.* n.d. Retrieved January 7, 2010, at www.pierre-gagnaire.com/francais/cdthis.htm.

Irvine, Martin. Georgetown University. "Postmodern," "Postmodernism," "Postmodernity." *The Po-Mo Page.* Web, 2004–2011. Retrieved October 11, 2007, at www.georgetown.edu/faculty/irvinem/technoculture/pomo.html. Retrieved April 8, 2011, at www9.georgetown.edu/faculty/irvinem/theory/pomo.html.

McGee, Harold. "Modern Cooking, Science, and the Erice Workshops on Molecular and Physical Gastronomy." *Curious Cook* (May 2008). Retrieved June 27, 2011, at www.curiouscook.com/site/erice-workshops.html.

This, Hervè. "The Art & Science of Molecular Gastronomy." American Culinary Federation Windy City Professional Culinarians educational seminar, Union League Club of Chicago. April 12, 2007.

Images

Alinea Menu. *Alinea Restaurant.* September 1, 2005. Courtesy of Chef Grant Achatz.

9

Design and Culinary Plate Archetypes

Design is a process—not a thing; it is a process of answering questions to create a solution. Culinary design is a method of investigation that is a relationship between the ingredients and the skills of the chef. The solution that we are trying to achieve is a successful plate presentation. This chapter considers plate presentation as a design process and examines some universal design terms and concepts.

Remember, in order to create successful plates, a cook must first have an automatic response to fundamental cooking processes and a developed recall of previous flavor affinities: a repertoire. Then, using a historical system, like the *culinary Art history* presented in this manual, to recall previous patterns of successful plates can greatly enhance contemporary design of food.

Archetypes are models that serve as patterns for similar work

Chefs and cooks use them all the time without calling them so. A picture of a plated dish is often provided to cooks so they may match a restaurant's presentation of the dish.

The *plate archetypes* presented in this manual are more theoretical, but they too represent a model for designing plates.

◎ CREATIVE CULINARY QUESTIONS

Design on plates happens on two levels. The first consideration level is flavor and the second is presentation. Chefs use different approaches to designing food; a chef will even use different methods at different times. Chapter 2 presented fundamental questions to create a successful plate:

In what food category is this design?

What is the desired price point of the design?

What type of service is used to deliver the design to the customer?

What type of menu is this food being designed for?

The next question that would logically follow from this list is:

What is the focus food of the plate design?

The focus food leads to the choices concerning sauce and accompanying *dishes* or ingredients. So the design process may be represented as follows:

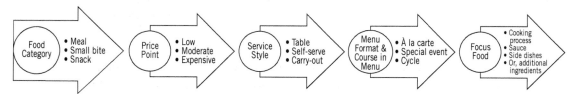

This is a very clear-cut method for developing a plate, or food design. However, experienced chefs do not strictly follow one method. The requirements of the food design are sometimes not considered first at all. Instead, a piece of serviceware or an ingredient in the market will cause the development of a dish. The next two chapters will explore different ways decisions are made about associating foods with a focus food.

Design is used in many specialized fields of industry and art; yet there are similarities in the way designers approach, consider, and see visual information. Recognizing patterns of visual information is essential to talking and thinking about design in an area. The way items are arranged in space is called a composition; in culinary, this is achieved through plating. Our compositions are called presentations. The 16 plate archetypes presented in the last four chapters are compositional patterns. Archetypes are a type of model on which similar type of designs are based; they serve as typical examples.

To describe the archetypal plate designs or any culinary presentation, it is useful to be able to recognize the effect of design elements and principles. It is less useful to think about these elements and principles as you are plating; design principles serve best during the evaluative phase. The language of design is a bridge between visual information and understanding.

◎ ELEMENTS OF DESIGN

The physical characteristics of products, such as paint or food ingredients, are elements of design. Design elements can also be created by the way products are manipulated or assembled.

Color

Color wheels have long been used to show relationships between colors. The most fundamental color wheels are based on a triangle of red, blue, and yellow.

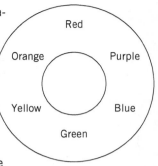

There are many hues between the colors in this wheel. Color hues that are next to each other are called analogous colors. An example of this type of color combinations can be seen in the bark of trees with many shades of brown. When gray is added to one of the hues on the color wheel, the result is called a tone. Complementary colors are colors directly across from each other. These combinations are often used for holiday themes; they can be seen in nature in such things as a purple flower with yellow stamen.

The natural color of ingredients offers a wide range of hues. It is never advisable to use artificial colors in the savory kitchen. It is often asserted that colors should be varied on a plate, which is not always true. Salads, for instance, can be beautiful in all green hues; but then the textures are varied. However, plates with color hues all from the brown family—tan, golden, chocolate—are often distressing. Plates that use tones of all one color or hues of analogous colors require greater sophistication in concept than plates with a variety of colors to be successful. The serviceware and the course before and after the tone-on-tone plate must emphasize that this was an intentional use. That is why beginning cooks are urged to vary colors on one plate.

Colors often suggest flavor; for example, a red might make a person think that a desert is strawberry or cherry. Flavor, remember, is the critical consideration for a cook; if you are adding something to a plate because of color, you are probably not working in the best possible way. Yet, interesting results can be achieved through the association of color and flavor that is unexpected. The Heinz Company did just that in the early 2000s when it released a innovative line of different-colored ketchup.

Texture / Pattern

Texture is a property inherent in all things. Texture can run through the whole of a substance or be simply a surface property—where the interior is a different texture. Texture is experienced in two ways: the look of an object is visual texture while the feel of an object is tactile texture.

The texture of things changes with such factors as temperature, moisture, and shape. Food science investigates these chemical changes in foods. Starches and gums increase thickness; heat makes proteins coagulate; emulsified fats add smoothness; different concentration of sugars when heated can change from syrupy to brittle. A cook knows many of these things without scientific experimentation through practice. Texture is a primary consideration in culinary compositions. It is an organizing element of culinary design; texture can be used to create shapes, lines, and patterns.

Shape / Form / Line

Shapes can be either organic, such as things found in nature, or geometric, such as circles and squares, like those found in buildings and products. A shape becomes a form when it is three-dimensional. When a chef cooks baby vegetables and presents them as they are, these are organic shapes. If a chef cuts the vegetables into different shapes like round slices or julienne, these are geometric shapes. However, if the chef purees the cooked vegetables and presses them into a mold to be turned out on the plate, then these are formed vegetables. The *Frames* and *styles* of Professional cuisine demonstrate that chefs have valued organic, geometric, and formed foods differently, depending on the style they are working in.

Formed ingredients should never sacrifice the optimal eating texture to be made to hold together in a mold. Likewise, ingredients should not be cut in a way that reduces their natural goodness; for instance, cutting meat against the grain will increase its toughness. Care must be used when deciding to cut or mold ingredients so that the value inherent in the natural product is not diminished. Consider a baby lamb rack—these are often fabricated as *Frenched* chops, which showcases the natural shape of the rack. If instead the meat was completely removed from the bone and cut into cubes, this would devalue this expensive cut. In other words, if you are using an expensive or unique ingredient, think seriously before you puree or cut it so that its original form is lost.

In art and design, a line has no depth—only width and length. Culinary lines almost always have a depth to them. Lines direct the eye in a composition. The way ingredients or *dishes* are arranged may create a line in culinary compositions; on a buffet platter, having clean curves or straight lines is essential to a good presentation. On plates, lines are more often created with sauces because there are not enough ingredients or *dishes* to create lines in the smaller space of plate although lines can be created in plate designs, such as when a chef fans out a sliced item. The important quality of a culinary line is that it is "clean"; this means that there are no unintentional jagged edges or hiccups in the slicing or placement of ingredients and that sauces are boldly laid down without smudges or unintentional drops.

FIGURE 9.1

Unordinary Cauliflower. Pictured here side by side are cauliflower and Romanesco. While people are generally very familiar with cauliflower, they are often not at all aware of Romanesco. This uniqueness, coupled with the intriguing form of Romanesco, is more greatly appreciated when served in flowerets than pureed.

Space—Height

Culinary space is framed by the edges of the plate. Thinking about how full a plate is or about the areas left between *dishes* or ingredients on a plate are spatial considerations. Although plates are often filled to the rim by customers at a buffet, empty areas, referred to as negative space, are essential in plate presentations. The empty spaces give value to the food presented.

In culinary compositions, almost every ingredient or *dish* presented on a plate has some dimension that rises from the flat surface. When chefs refer to height, they are talking about things that are "standing." A lamb chop laid down has dimension off the plate, but this is not considered to add height. Instead, if you were to lean this lamb chop against a mound of potatoes, so that the tip of the bone points up, then the chop would be considered as adding height. This is one of the differences between a Face plate and a BUFF plate—both of which are often used to present a focus food and two side dishes.

 ## PRINCIPLES OF DESIGN

Principles are patterns of thought that prove useful in understanding and working in design. Because human brains share similarities in the way they organize visual information, certain "looks" appeal across cultures and time. The way that pieces of a composition relate to the whole composition can be described using design principles.

Scale and Proportion

The scale of a work is its overall size; the parts of the work relate to each other and to the totality of the work in proportion. In culinary presentations, the scale of the work is determined by serving method. If the chef and cooks are plating in the kitchen, then the scale of the work is determined by the serving-plate size.

The size of the *dishes* and ingredients are proportional to the serving plate and each other. Traditionally, the focus is set by the largest dish or ingredient, left whole, on the serving plate. The other dishes or ingredients are then sized in proportion to this focus food. If too much of one dish or ingredient, or if too much food, is put on a service plate, it is said to be out of proportion. This relates to balancing a composition.

Visual Weight

Visual weight can be given to elements through the use of proportion, emphasis, pattern, or placement. In culinary presentations, emphasis is usually given to a *dish* or ingredient by size, placement, or color. For instance, the focus food is generally the largest item on the plate, and when the plate is set before a diner, the focus food is facing, or nearest, the diner. Or, imagine a plate where all the ingredients are shades of white and the sauce is brilliant red; then, despite the size of all the other foods on the plate, it will be the sauce that is the emphasis. Sometimes, large garnishes that are placed on top of stacked ingredients become the emphasized food. Think of a long fried chip placed on top of a presentation—is it the first thing that you want the eye to go to?

This is an important consideration when using one of the stacked archetypes because the top of the stack is emphasized by its height. Having this emphasis will change the way sauce is placed around the stack; if a pattern is drawn in the sauce surrounding the stack, it may compete with the focus of the stack. Patterns create an emphasis.

FIGURE 9.2

Portion Proportion. In this image, 4 ounces of carrot puree are shown on plates ranging in circumference from 12 inches to 6 inches. Does the size of plate make you think about the puree differently?

Patterns

Pattern is the repetition of certain shapes in an organized way. It may be the use of a repeating motif across the whole background or alternating shapes on a line. In culinary presentation, patterns are generally made by repeating *dishes* or ingredients around a focus food to form a border or borders that are created with sauces. There are random patterns in free-style mounds of vegetables or starches, but we think of these as texture in culinary. Patterned repetitions are often used in Classical platters or on Nouvelle plates such as the Sun, or in sauce around a single Island design.

Generally, patterns are stronger visual attractions than texture alone because they rely on color and shape repetitions as well as texture. For example, the way a sauce is plated is dependent on texture, and the presentation of sauces creates patterns on the plate.

Arrangements and Balance

The arrangement of elements within a composition can be described as symmetrical or asymmetrical. There are different types of symmetry, but the two most often associated with plate designs are reflective and radial. Reflective symmetry describes a design that, when divided down the middle, both sides are exactly the same; radial symmetry describes a design where all the rays extending from a center point are the same. Classical patterns and Nouvelle plates are most likely to have reflective or radial symmetry. A symmetrical composition is balanced; there is equal visual weight on both sides of the presentation because of the placement of ingredients.

In an asymmetrical composition, each side is different. Asymmetrical arrangements can be balanced using pattern or emphasis to provide visual weight. Plate presentations done on serviceware that is not round are often asymmetrical, but through the use of pattern and placement are balanced in visual weight. This is true for the archetypes of elemental, linear, course within a course, and deconstruction plates.

By constructing an imaginary grid over a plate, you can see if the visual weight is balanced in the frame of the plate. Chef Keith Keogh and the Culinary Team USA in 1993 checked the balance of their plates by tying strings between two set of cups, then positioning the cups to form a string "x" at the center of the plate (Keogh 1999, 251). This allowed them to check if there was equal visual weight in all four quadrants of a round plate even if the arrangement was not symmetrical.

A nine-sectioned grid is more useful for rectangular or square plates. If a square or rectangular piece of serviceware is divided into thirds vertically and horizontally, the grid

FIGURE 9.3

Plate Balance. In this image, a BUFF plate has been set up with cups and a string "x." Look at each quadrant of the plate. Is there an equal amount of food in each area?

that results approximates the golden ratio. The golden ratio was extrapolated out of nature from such occurrences as the spiral of shells and the ratio of parts of a body to the whole body. It is a mathematical relationship that approximates one-third to two-thirds to the whole.

Now consider how food is often placed on such a plate. Are the dishes placed at the foci of the grid? Or in the boxes created in the middle of the grid? There is not only one way that is best. Instead, this is simply a design tool to help you think about what works best. It is wrong to think that you should fit your presentations to an exact model, but by considering the model your presentations might be adjusted to work better. Using alignment to create structured or suggested rows gives a sense of unity to a linear presentation.

Balance, of course, relates to more than spatial arrangements for culinary presentations. Flavors, cooking methods, and serving sizes must also be balanced in proportion to each element of a plate. Each style of plating has different guidelines for how this is achieved, and can be reviewed in relation to each individual style.

Arrangements also pertain to the number of elements presented on a plate or in a grouping on a plate. Oftentimes in culinary presentations, the use of an odd number is suggested as better than an even number. Look at the following examples based on Fan designs to see if you agree.

FIGURE 9.4

Odd versus Even. The left-hand image uses an odd number of vegetables on either side of the radiating fan; the right-hand image uses an even number. Does one picture look more appealing than the other?

Unity

In a composition, unity is what brings together all the elements. Design unity can be achieved with placement, proximity (placing objects that are related close together), continuation (using lines or placement of elements so that the viewer's eye will continue along a desired direction), or repetition (using a shape or color multiple times in different places of a composition).

In culinary evaluations, unity has come to be used almost exclusively in terms of placement; a unified presentation is one that is all drawn together in the center of the plate. This is, in part, because of the wide acceptance of the BUFF archetype. This plate presentation was in fact designed to create balance, unity, visual flow, and focus.

But, repetition is used to unite the ingredients in Mound or Deconstruction archetypes. Many times sauce is used to unify presentations not only in terms of binding flavors but also in placement that makes the eye continue around a grouping of food. The line of a sauce placement might encircle a presentation; or, the dots of sauce might, through repetition, unify a more dispersed presentation.

However, the most important factor of culinary unity is flavor. In other words, it is the understanding of why all these ingredients or *dishes* are put together on a plate, which always has the same underlying truth: Together they are more delicious than they would be served alone. Unity is the understanding that the whole is greater than the sum of its parts. The synergy of ingredients working together produces a larger effect than any individual ingredient could alone.

Unity can be thought of as harmonious flavor combinations and also as compatible parts that are arranged in an orderly way to make the presentation easier for the eye to read.

Variety

The relationship between unity and variety is not antonymous but rather complementary. A series of hot days followed by a day of cool breezes is refreshing because of the contrast. Variety makes unity interesting; too much variety leads to visual chaos in designs. Variety is achieved by varying textures, shapes, and colors in a composition, as well as flavors in culinary presentations.

Contrast is a big part of variety. A crunchy texture feels crunchier next to smooth textures than next to other crisp ingredients. Colors that are opposite on the color wheel, placed next to each other, look brighter. Contrast and wide variance are not considered as essential in Classical and Nouvelle styles but are more important characteristics in Fusion, New American, and Global styles.

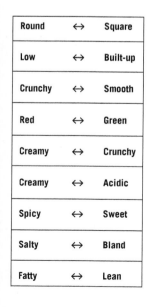

Round	↔	Square
Low	↔	Built-up
Crunchy	↔	Smooth
Red	↔	Green
Creamy	↔	Crunchy
Creamy	↔	Acidic
Spicy	↔	Sweet
Salty	↔	Bland
Fatty	↔	Lean

Balance is essential between unity and variety. If ingredients or *dishes* are too varied, the presentation is not easy to perceive as belonging together; if ingredients or dishes are too similar, the presentation is perceived as dull and bland. In general, a plate of all round shapes would be poor in design, but what if the shape of new potatoes and peas are presented together because they were at their peak in the spring market? Remember: Design in food happens on two levels. The first consideration level is flavor and the second is presentation.

A list of complementary attributes of *dishes* and ingredients is helpful in thinking about balance.

Notice that there are flavor pairs in the list—not just design elements—because plate design elements must always be kept in the context of flavor. Changing the cut of an ingredient does affect flavor. The visual messages of the *dishes* and ingredients also serve to create flavor as well as contain it. Texture is, in fact, the intersection between flavor and appearance often made through cooking techniques.

Sometimes in a menu one course will emphasize a certain quality, such as creamy, so that the next course of crunchy highlights a playful contrast. Either of these plates out of the context of the menu might seem overwhelming in creaminess or crunchiness served alone. Balance relates not simply to a plate but to the course placement of the plate as well.

Presentations do, in the final stages of culinary expression, create another layer of flavor by further sequencing how foods will be combined and perceived by the diner. Flavor is expressed through elements of food presentation—food choices, arrangement, color, and texture.

◎ CONSIDERATIONS IN CULINARY DESIGN

The elements and principles of design give us a language to talk about the look of food presentations. There are also some decisions we make while plating that are less easily seen; these I have grouped together as considerations. The ability of the kitchen and service staff, the perception of the diner, and the nature of the ingredients, all influence the design principles expressed in plating.

Serviceability

Once a plate is finished, it must be served to a customer. If the presentation is easily upset by being moved, then it does not have the right serviceability. It is not effective because by the time the diner perceives the plate, it is flawed. This might happen if ingredients or *dishes* are stacked or balanced in an exaggerated or unstable way. This is one of the reasons that soup is now poured at the table into a bowl; the center garnish is displayed intact before liquid might cause it to move or float. This method of serving soups also keeps the soup much hotter, which makes it a better design not only in look but function.

More commonly, upsets occur when there is not enough empty space around the edge of a plate; this empty space was traditionally marked off as the rim on a plate but in newer styles of serviceware, rims might not exist. If the presentation does not have this empty edge, the presentation is likely to be pushed by the servers' fingers or a plate cover. Empty space is important in presentations to highlight the value of the *dishes* or ingredients on the plate; but also, empty space is important around the outside edge to increase serviceability.

Serviceability also refers to the way a customer will eat the presentation. If a tall presentation is served on a small plate, when the diner begins to eat the food it will topple off the plate. Or, if food is put into smaller serviceware that is part of a larger plate, then the customer must have the right silverware to get into the smaller containers. If these smaller containers are meant to be picked up and sauces from other *dishes* on the plate have run under them, then there is a risk the customers will drop sauce onto themselves. Presentations must be fitted not only to the serviceware used but also fitted to how a customer is expected to use the serviceware.

Notice in all these examples that the best solutions for serving presentations function at two levels. The design increases the attractiveness of the presentation and also furthers the pleasure of eating the presentation.

Serviceability also relates to how easily a presentation can be done by the cooks during service. If a presentation is beautiful, and it serves and eats well but cannot be done over and over in a timely fashion, it is not effective. Thus, serviceability relates presentations to the ability of wait staff, the diners, and the cooks to interact well with a design.

Degree of Difficulty

In culinary competitions or other evaluations of presentations, points are often awarded for achieving a certain level of technical difficulty. In other words, a plate of *dishes* that demonstrate mastery of a variety of techniques is given more points than a straightforward plate of dishes. Consider a Face plate design of cooked meat, buttered sliced carrots, and mashed potatoes.

If, instead, I turn the carrots and pipe the mashed potatoes into heightened swirls, which I then brown off under the broiler with cheese, I have demonstrated increased technical ability. I then might rearrange the Face into a BUFF plate. This demonstrates more technical ability. But, the question I must always ask myself is: What did it do to the flavors and serviceability of the food?

Increasing the complexity of a plate or in the preparation of *dishes* and ingredients can be thrilling for a cook. It fuels our imagination and demonstrates our professional know-how. But there must be an understanding of why the increased complexity is important. Paramount to any increase in complexity is an understanding of why it is being done and having the technical competency to achieve it. Styles in Professional cuisine have addressed this issue differently. Simplicity and complexity are much like unity and variety—they are not antonymous but complementary. A balance is achieved in the best presentations; for example, complex flavors are often best showcased in simpler designs.

Charles Mingus, a renowned jazz musician and composer of the twentieth century, is credited with having said, "Anyone can make the simple complicated. Creativity is making the complicated simple." There should always be underlying understandings of why you choose to present *dishes* and ingredients differently. The goal of working through the exercises of this book is to help you clarify your reasons for culinary creativity. In the next two chapters, the way that the ingredients and culinary processes guide your decisions is examined. The way you ultimately decide to express flavor can be influenced and inspired by many factors.

QUERIES & INQUIRIES

1. What is design?
2. What are the two principal design concerns on a plate?
3. What is the basic sequence of questions used to guide plate design?
4. What are the elements of design listed in this chapter? Are there other design elements that you think are also important to consider when designing a plate?

5. When deciding to give a different texture or shape to an ingredient, what are important considerations?

6. What is the difference between an element of design and a principle of design?

7. What does the term *visual weight* describe? How can visual weight be created on a plate?

8. Choose three pictures of plated food that include the edges of the plate and create a grid over each image. Are the plates visually balanced? If they are not, how could they be re-presented to create balance?

9. Is it important to have an odd number of elements in a plate design rather than an even number?

10. How can unity of design be achieved on a plate?

11. What does the term *serviceability* describe?

CITATION AND REFERENCE MATERIALS

Aimone, Steven. *Design! A Lively Guide to Design Basics for Artists & Craftspeople*. New York: Lark Books, a division of Sterling Publishing Co. Inc. 2007.

De Santis, Ronald. "B.U.F.F.-Up on Food Presentation." *The National Culinary Review* (Feb. 1998): 6–10.

Keogh, Keith, and Culinary Team USA. New Currents in American Cuisine. Illinois: Cahners Publishing Company, 1993.

Keogh, Keith. "The Art of Plate Presentation." *The National Culinary Review* (Sept. 1999): 30–34.

Lawson, Bryan. *How Designers Think: The Design Process Demystified*, 4th ed. Oxford: Elsevier Ltd., 2006.

Lidwell, William, Kritina Holden, and Jill Butler. *Universal Principles of Design*. Massachusetts: Rockport Publishers, Inc., 2003.

10

Looking for Inspiration

If you live within a small community where change happens over generations and people have a very similar way of living, you do not need to look for much inspiration in the way you serve food. The way meals are served and the type of foods that are eaten remain fairly constant within a person's lifetime. However, almost none of us live in such communities anymore. Professional cuisine serves a much larger community, with a significant rate of change experienced in one professional's lifetime.

THE WORLD AT LARGE

Novelty, creativity, and originality have long been important values for professional chefs. Even within Classical style, where such values are not primary, Chef Escoffier stated in his 1907 introduction to Le Guide, "We ourselves should seek new approaches that have been adapted to the customs and needs of our time" (Escoffier 1982, xiv).

Sometimes a chef will have an event to prepare for that suggests a theme, such as when you plan a menu for a wedding or birthday party, or the event might be centered on a specific person or place. For example, it is said that the dish *Pompano en Papillote* was developed by Restaurateur Jules Alciatore for a New Orleans banquet honoring a famous balloonist. A paper envelope, enclosing the ingredients, would puff up as it cooked, resembling a balloon. French chefs had used this technique previously, but it was the association given by Alciatore that popularized it in the United States (Mariani 1994, 240).

Often, culinary inspiration is not something you think about until after it strikes. In other words, you are going about your work or enjoying your time off and a vision of a plate or an idea for a dish just seems to come into your head. This might be due to the fact that the more a person enjoys something, the more time they spend thinking about it. This strengthens associations in your mind that trace back to that subject of enjoyment. If you're a professional chef, food is often on your mind. Deepening your involvement in cultural events expands your connections to creative food.

◎ MIMICRY

A very clear example of how mental associations lead to culinary creativity is the production of figurative foods. These are foods that are shaped into a figure, such as an animal, person or buildings to associate the dining experience with another important thing or event.

Another part of why figurative foods are a good example of associative creativity is a personal one. Since I have been thinking and researching about food presentations for the last seven years, I came to know that during banquets given in the Medieval and Renaissance periods of France and Italy, foods were molded to resemble other foods during the days that meat was forbidden due to religious laws—such as fish being ground and reshaped to resemble a poultry dish. These were called *illusion foods* because they gave the illusion of one flavor but were indeed a different flavor.

I also learned that during very important banquets, food was often shaped into elaborate designs to honor a royal guest. These large food sculptures were frequently themed around Roman mythology, famous battles or births. Often made of sugar, they were carried into the dining hall between courses and called *entremets* (see Chapter 3).

FIGURE 10.1

Figurative and Illusion Foods. This image shows a hamburger plate with a side of potatoes. The burger is an example of an illusion food because it is made of soy protein instead of the traditional ground beef. The potatoes shaped as men are an example of a figurative food—food shaped to represent a character, symbol, or place.

Literally meaning between the courses, the word later evolved to be a course in Table menus. This deepened my understanding of the role of an entremets course used to punctuate and delight between more substantial courses.

Furthermore, during the same period, foods would sometimes be shaped and filled with other things to surprise the guests when cut open (see Chapter 3). There were things like pie shells baked empty and filled with live birds, so that when cut open in the room, the birds would fly out, or ground molded meat shaped like a deer that "bled" red wine. But the idea of shaping foods for delight and surprise was something I had experienced in my own career, such as hard boiled eggs being shaped like penguins on a cold buffet or making givrés, which are frozen fruits filled with a sorbet of the fruit's pulp.

Kaiseki, a formal Japanese dining experience, utilizes this type of symbolism in choosing ingredients and plates that evoke meanings tied to literary and cultural references. These references may or may not be discerned by a particular guest at the meal, but for those who make the associations, the meal holds a deeper and richer meaning (Riccardi 2003, 90).

These foods involve symbolism that might be figurative or conceptual; they rely on the diner making associations outside of the eating experience to other types of experience such as a well-known event or cultural phenomenon. In many ways this is the type of the creativity that is used by Techno-emotive chefs.

Knowing the nature of different ingredients, then, can inspire a chef to use one ingredient to mimic another ingredient such as corn ice cream shaped in an asparagus mold. It is a sophisticated playfulness that increases a chef's creativity based on experiences of not only ingredients but also culture at large.

◎ MENTAL MAPS

You can help strengthen these associations that give inspiration about food by working to create mental maps. When visiting a new location, you come to discover different neighborhoods that are good for shopping or going out; these neighborhood maps fuse into a more complete web of the location's layout. The culinary "neighborhoods" are ingredients, technology, and culinary traditions.

The preceding chapters have provided a set of questions to place presentations within a context of service and menu. The *culinary Art history* outlined how chefs have previously designed presentations in the different styles of service and menus. The question, then, is, how do chefs make decisions about what, rather than how, to present? Chefs in each style shared ways of looking at culinary creativity, but each style had different emphasis areas of inspiration. For example, Classical menus were inspired by a set of luxury foods, the regularity of geometric shapes, and ordered principles regarding food choices. Nouvelle menus' inspiration came from local products, seasonal affinities, and hearth-based traditions. Fusion style menus' inspiration was the inclusion of "exotic" elements into established professional cuisine. Techno-emotive menus have elements of food-processing technology as inspiration.

Sources that chefs regularly consider when choosing *dishes* or ingredients to plate together are found in the culinary "neighborhoods" or inspirational sets. Decisions are often based on associations within a set of established relationships. Inspirational sets are like mental maps that start at one point and branch out to many possible links. This can be compared to creating a culinary web in your mind with different search engines that can be used to answer a question.

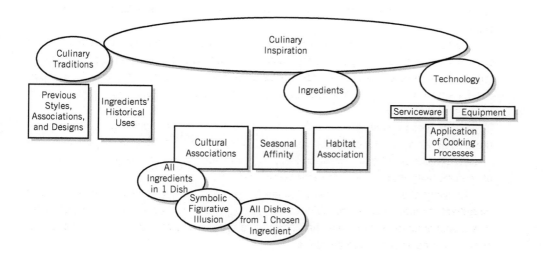

◎ INGREDIENTS

It is unusual for a chef to create *dishes* or platings without any ingredients that need to be used from the walk-in or as leftovers from other preparations. Most times it is these ingredients that anchor the development of a dish or plate. Regardless of where the first ingredient comes from, it is generally through associations that the rest of the ingredients are chosen. Ingredients are the prime value of culinary creativity. Ingredients are often grouped by the season, a habitat, or a cultural tradition; maps of these different groups, or sets, will overlap, creating a culinary web.

Seasonal Affinity

The ingredients that are in season at the same time in the same geographical area have long been considered as the starting point for menus. Ingredients that are available in the same season generally share an affinity of flavor. Depending on where you live, the links, or ingredients in the market, will be different. To begin to use this search engine, you need to create lists of ingredients for each season, available where you are working. Here is an example for the fall season:

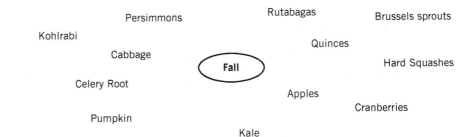

Persimmons   Rutabagas   Brussels sprouts

Kohlrabi   Quinces

Cabbage   **Fall**   Hard Squashes

Celery Root   Apples   Cranberries

Pumpkin

Kale

Simply by taking the time to search online or visit a seasonal market to make such lists will strengthen your culinary creativity.

Habitat Associations

Another series of inspirational sets that are useful are based on the natural environment of an ingredient. Ingredients that are found or generally grow together also share flavor affinities. This is not to suggest foraging for wild edibles, many of which are protected by law and require vast knowledge to harvest safely, but rather a way of thinking about choosing ingredients when shopping or ordering.

Here is an example using a forested area:

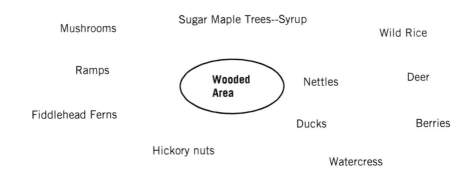

Sugar Maple Trees--Syrup

Mushrooms   Wild Rice

Ramps   **Wooded Area**   Nettles   Deer

Fiddlehead Ferns   Ducks   Berries

Hickory nuts   Watercress

This is not to say that all the associations fit with each other, but considering such groupings when combining ingredients is more likely to lead to successful flavor pairings.

FIGURE 10.3

A Lakeside Dish using a Duo Design. In this image, duck, a water fowl, is presented two ways. A pan-seared duck breast is accompanied with a watercress salad that is garnished with wild rice and cranberries. The watercress, wild rice, and cranberries all grow in similar water environments.

Cultural Traditions

Ingredients that have long been combined within certain cultural traditions have stood the test of time. They are proven flavors that work well together. Choosing ingredients and then creating associated flavors within one traditional cuisine will create another series of inspirational sets. You can begin by creating lists of dishes from different traditions. This not only provides a starting point for ingredient maps but also shows ingredients that are associated in different cuisines. Once again, it should be seen that a repertoire of dishes is foundational for success.

The easiest way to begin is to choose a dish from outside your own food tradition that you have eaten often and list out the important flavor ingredients. Here is an example based on bouillabaisse, a fish soup-stew from the South of France:

◆ Tomatoes

◆ Onion

◆ Garlic

◆ Saffron

◆ Seafood

◆ Fennel

◆ Orange

◆ Red hot pepper

Another way to approach these types of sets are by choosing one ingredient and making a list of all the dishes you know that contain the ingredient. Here is an example using the all-American ingredient: Bacon.

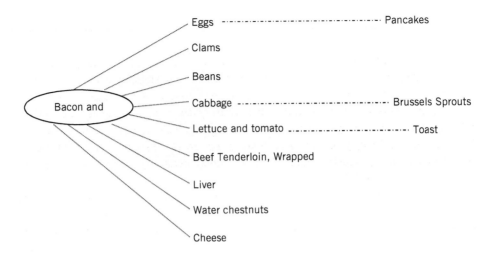

This approach uses cultural traditions as can be seen in the cabbage and bacon pair, from a favorite Irish dish, or uses the work of other chefs, such as the idea of bacon and water chestnuts (with chicken livers) used to make Rumaki, thought to be the creation of restaurateur Vic Bergeron of the original Trader Vic's restaurant in San Francisco (Rumaki 2002). Looking at successful dishes from other chefs is one of the fundamental ways to develop because cooks all begin by copying when working under a chef. Cooks make copies of an already-developed *dish,* and eventually—after working under many chefs who influence their growth—they extract a personal style.

One of the most beautiful dishes I have seen that came from associative work like this was a plating of bacon-wrapped monkfish served with buckwheat blini, sunny-side-up quail egg, and maple syrup foam.

Two other methods of relating ingredients merit mentioning. The first relates simply to color; ingredients that are in the same color family, such as all green vegetables, seem to go together well. I hesitate in mentioning this because it is an error to begin by considering color when plating; yet, it might prove useful to create lists of color-associated ingredients. The second method works by associating an ingredient to other dishes of the same ingredient over historical periods. For example, corn was used by early settlers of the United States to make johnnycakes, a type of thin corn pancake done on a griddle. In the early twentieth century, popped corn became popular, so that now watching a movie and eating popcorn is almost synonymous. And, in the 1980s it became very popular to make corncob stock. So by knowing these three historical uses of corn to make different dishes, a chef might be able to better create a Trio plate; or perhaps it might suggest something like popcorn-crusted lake trout with a broth-like sauce built from a corncob stock garnished with a very thin white corn johnnycake.

◎ TECHNOLOGY

The word *technology* and its meaning evolved from Greek language, originally referring to an applied system of skill. Later the word was more closely associated with the applied sciences and mechanical arts in relation to manufacturing and industry. Just as Art became a specialized field removed from the craft workshop, so, too, was technology. The craftshop could not keep pace with developments in industry generating new technologies. The kitchen, though, remains a craft workshop, an *atelier*, which uses technologies developed not only by industry but also from the chefs interacting in exploratory ways with the technology (Risatti 2007).

A great example of this is the use of the whipped cream canister. When whipping heavy cream into a stiff peak, the action of beating with a whip changes the molecular bonds of the cream and forces air into the milk fat, creating a foamed emulsion. A whipped cream canister creates a foamed emulsion when the lever is pressed, allowing the pressurized mixture of cream and gas to expand out. European industries have been manufacturing nitrous oxide cream chargers since the mid-twentieth-century, and correspondingly, chefs used them to put whipped cream mixtures on desserts. In the 1990s, Chef Ferran Adrià used this canister to produce foams that were not based on heavy cream. Savory foams, created with bases other than whipped cream, now are used in kitchens across the world. Thus, existing technologies and kitchen equipment considered in new ways can provide culinary creativity.

When using any new equipment or when considering using equipment in a new way—**safety is always the first consideration**. Equipment or ingredients used without prior research and understanding can not only cause accidents or illness but also death. Collaboration with a scientist or a manufacturer is required to understand the limits of creativity.

Cooking processes are applied science. Chefs have long used scientific knowledge in the production of food. Refrigeration, freezing, and new fuel sources for heating are obvious ways cooking is affected by technology—applied scientific theory. Since the time of Carême, chefs have thought about themselves as participating in the art and science of culinary practice. Contemporary chefs may study food science to deepen their understandings of what is happening on a molecular level in the kitchen. While working in the kitchen, the fundamental understanding is, of course, how cooking processes affect food on the surface level. Changing how these practices are applied to different ingredients is a great source of creativity. The next chapter will explore these possibilities in more depth.

The serviceware chefs chose to present food on is also part of culinary technology. Before the technological advances took place that allowed for the widespread manufacture of ceramic serviceware, food was eaten off of trenchers. Trenchers were commonly made of slices of hardened bread or wood. This influenced the way dishes were cooked. For example, dishes such as ragouts, which are very saucy, did not become popular until ceramic plates were in common use.

Acclaimed chefs will sometimes collaborate with designer to create new forms. Chef Thomas Keller spurred commercial production of serving pieces and trays that could hold small cones upright, as the now famous French Laundry salmon tartare cornets became widely popular. In Techno-emotive style, serving utensils are often designed to fit the serving of a particular dish.

The wisdom of earlier practices are inspiring new thoughts about presentations. Planked fish, especially salmon, was a traditional dish of First Nation people adapted by European settlers to cook fish in ovens. Chefs have translated these practices into Professional cuisine with cedar planks to cook and serve fish portions. Ethiopian dishes are generally served on top of a sourdough flatbread, injera; and, leaves, such as those of banana trees, are used as plates in various parts of the world. Changing what food is served on changes not only the presentation but also the way a chef thinks about food preparation.

Thus, culinary technology can be considered not only as the way chefs use kitchen equipment and tools but also as the system of skills and knowledge used in cooking methods and processes, as well as the serviceware that chefs choose to present food. Thinking about any one of these three areas can inspire a new way to see plating.

◎ CULINARY CREATIVITY: A SHARED MEANING

Culinary creativity is not something that is uniquely personal. It is based on associations and traditions. The results of any culinary creativity must relate not only to the abilities of the kitchen and wait staff but also to the diners at the table. It is about participating in an established community as well as furthering the development of the culinary community. The *dishes* and designs of chefs influence other chefs; the styles of Professional cuisine were and are relative to each other.

Just as psychologists might use word association to help expose the personality of the subconscious mind, chefs can use culinary association to imagine the personality of flavors. The real point of creating lists of associations is not to have paper references but rather to create a culinary web in your mind. So that when provided with an opportunity, your mind immediately begins to make associations that allow you to develop a *dish* or plate. It is the process of making the lists that is more important than the lists themselves.

Inspiration is found through engaging with world culture, culinary traditions, and ingredients. A student of the culinary arts should be able to recognize historical designs and use them as influences for contemporary work. A chef, throughout her career, grows by extending these associations of ingredients, technology, and traditions.

QUERIES & INQUIRIES

1. Where do chefs find inspiration for food design?

2. What are the inspirational sets suggested in this chapter? Are there other areas of association that you have used or seen used?

3. Draw a mental map of ingredients that are available during the same season in your area.

4. Draw a mental map of ingredients based on associations in nature or in a culinary tradition.

5. Choose an ingredient and list all the dishes you know that feature that ingredient. Examine the other ingredients of the dishes in your list. Do these other ingredients form any associations of their own?

6. Has learning how to use a new technology ever influenced your cooking? What technology was it? How did you apply it?

7. How does serviceware influence plate presentations? Create a plate design on a standard 9- to 12-inch round plate; now re-plate the design on a different-shaped plate. Did you have to change the design to fit the new serviceware? Does the re-presentation change the flavor or serviceability of the design?

CITATION AND REFERENCE MATERIALS

"Background and Clarification of Nitrous Chargers for Whipped Cream." *Creamright*. © 2001–2011. Retrieved May 2, 2011, at www.creamright.com/history.html.

Escoffier, Auguste. *Le Guide Culinaire*. Trans. H.L. Cracknell and R.J. Kaufmann. New York: Mayflower Books, 1982.

Keller, Thomas. *The French Laundry Cookbook*. New York: Artisan, 1999.

Mariani, Jon F. *The Dictionary of American Food and Drink*. New York: William Morrow and Company, 1994.

Riccardi, Victoria Abbott. *Untangle My Chopsticks, a Culinary Sojourn in Kyoto*. New York: Broadway Books, 2003.

Risatti, Howard. *A Theory of Craft*. The University of North Carolina Press, 2007.

"Rumaki." Epicurious.com. *Gourmet* (March 2002). © 2011 Condé Nast Digital. Retrieved May 2, 2011, at www.epicurious.com/recipes/food/views/Rumaki-106255.

Strong, Roy. *Feast: A History of Grand Eating*. Copyright Oman Productions Orlando: Harcourt, Inc., 2002.

Wheaton, Barbara Ketcham. *Savoring the Past: the French Kitchen and Table from 1300 to 1789*. New York: Touchstone Book edition, published by Simon & Schuster, 1996.

11

Plating the Styles

Defining what a meal should be sets the menu structure and service style. This is what underlies a change of style in Professional cuisine. The archetypal plate designs within each style are visual manifestations of such changes. This is what a chef sees in presentations: an expression of flavor fitted within a style, which is based on menu and service.

A change in the idea of what a meal should be changes both how menus are structured and how meals are served. This, then, is what changes a *Frame* in the *culinary Art history*. Subsequently, a style within a Frame changes when service remains fairly constant but the courses of the menu alter in concept and thus presentation. Menu items are affected by changes in sources of inspiration, foods that are emphasized, and cooking processes. Looking back at the style changes in the Plate Frame, this is evident in the language used to write menu descriptions, for example, small plate menus. It was a change in the concept of what a course should be that resulted in the presentation of small plates. Therefore, the look of a presentation, as represented by the archetypal plate design, is a reflection of these underlying changes in professional beliefs.

The menu sets the parameters of design for the archetypal plates. Further constraints are set by the specific course within the menu where the plate is to fit. Certain courses are traditionally linked to some ingredients or types of preparations, such as soup—it is a course listing as well as a preparation. In the beginning of Classical style, remember, there was a course listing of Roasts, which eventually became the main course in later Classical menus. Although other types of preparations are eventually used as main courses, roasted meats remain associated with the main course. Thus, there exists within Professional cuisine a link between ingredient choices and how they are prepared to fit a style's menu.

Considering the five styles of Professional cuisine, it is possible to link certain types of sauces, preparation methods, and garnishing techniques to plate designs.

SAUCE AND PLATE DESIGNS

When you have chosen a focus ingredient for a plate, what do you think of next? The most common answer is how that ingredient will be cooked. Of course, if you thought of a spice, the answer would be different, such as, how will I showcase this flavor? This is one of the biggest differences between Techno-emotive style and the other five styles. Techno-emotive considerations often start by conceptualizing a flavor rather than an ingredient. Global style's starting point is generally an ingredient, while Classical, Nouvelle, New American, and Fusion styles' plates generally begin with a focus food or *dish*. This is why, in more modern styles, a repertoire is not emphasized, yet the most successful modern chefs have usually had an extensive repertoire that serves as part of their mental culinary web.

Before you can successfully conceptualize expressing a flavor in a new medium, or even create a new expression of an ingredient, you must understand a *dish* that has that flavor or ingredient in it. So the questions to begin with are: What is the focus food, and how will it be prepared?

The preparation method, then, generally leads to a sauce choice. This is most obvious for the cooking methods of braising and stewing, where the sauce is part of the process; other cooking methods also suggest sauce relationships. Any cooking method that leaves behind juices suggests a sauce built on those juices. For instance, roasting suggests the accompanying jus lié or gravy built from the fond. Cooking methods that do not leave behind any essences, such as grilling or steaming, lead to independent sauce choices. Each Professional style has expanded the sauce repertoire; examining the types of sauces used in the Professional styles will help make this clear.

Classic	Nouvelle	Fusion	New American	Global
Béchamel	Stock reductions with wine and aromatics	Glazes	Vinegar based	Juices
Velouté	Coulis	Salsas	Barbeque	Essences
Espagnole	Beurre Blanc	Chutneys	Frothy emulsions	Waters
Hollandaise	Cream reductions	Broth-like	Gravies	Foam
Mayonnaise		Soy based	Flavored oils	Puree-like
Tomato		Paste based	Syrups	Frozen
Broken butters		Gastrique		Gel / emulsions
Compound butters				
Chaud-froid				

This table shows sauce categories similar in concept to the Classical "mother" sauces. Please note that it is *absolutely not true* that chefs working in one style will only use the sauces listed under that style. Rather, the table listings show sauce categories that are emphasized in the style or were developed during that style. For example, dried or semi-dried powders, which are not listed, are also used like sauces on plates from New American style forward. If the primary purpose of a sauce is to add moisture to a plate, then powders are not sauces, but if a sauce is considered as an element of plating that will never be eaten alone and deepens or contrasts the other flavors on a plate, then powders might be called dry sauces.

The type of sauce that is going to be used has an important influence on the serviceware used for plating; because each of these sauces has different consistencies, they require different types of surfaces or containment. So the next consideration is how these sauces are often plated; these types of considerations will, in turn, guide choices about serviceware.

	Classic	Nouvelle	Fusion/New American	Global
Typical Textures	Viscous liquid Smooth	Viscous liquid Smooth	Frothy Unthickened liquid Chunky Syrupy Oily "Dried"	Unthickened liquid Syrupy Foamy Very viscous liquid Crystals—beads "Dried"
Typical Plating	Spooned over food	Spooned on plate under / around food, dotted, dragged, drawn with	Spooned on plate or food Wet and dry lines Surrounded by unthickened sauces possibly with oil droplets	Droplets Wet and dry lines Surrounded by unthickened sauces possibly with oil droplets Smears Brushes Pulled valleys Mohawks Scattered Pulled "purees"

The emphasis on sauce as a major component of a dish decreased after Nouvelle style. Oftentimes, sauces were dots or lines and not of a consistency to cover *dishes*. This was a shift in the defining of a dish; whereas previously, the sauce and the focus food were linked in the menu description, in later styles, all ingredients are listed to describe dishes on the menu. Serviceware that had a rim and was round was no longer needed to present these newer style sauces and dishes; thus, the look of plates changed from one of geometric shapes and symmetry to more abstract and linear arrangements.

Interestingly, it was at this point that cookbooks began to have close-up shots of presentations; often, the edges of the serviceware were not evident in the photo at all. The focus on ingredient display in plating changed the chef's view of *dishes*. The process of visually presenting flavor became as important as the cooking processes. Plating was used as another process to create a *dish*.

◎ PREPARATION METHODS AND PLATE DESIGN

Certain culinary processes and plate designs seem to fit together. Cooking methods, applying heat to ingredients, are only one category of culinary processes. There are also culinary techniques, such as making a puree or custard, as well as raw processes and knife cuts. Culinary processes are all the techniques and methods chefs use to prepare ingredients and, as previously mentioned, how these processes are associated on a plate is sometimes lost when they are learned separately, abstracted from a *dish* or presentation.

Examining the archetypal plate designs shows that certain processes are emphasized within each style, as demonstrated in the following chart. It would be erroneous to think that these processes are only used in the style they are listed under, or that other processes not listed are not used; instead, the chart serves as a starting point for considering how chefs create flavor differently within the styles.

Classic	Nouvelle	Fusion	New American	Global
Grinding	Wrapping	Sautéed	Layering	Gel—cube, pipe, sheet
Molding	Shingling	Using a specialty oven	Savory custard	Savory frozen
Wrapping	Savory mousses	—such as tandoor or pit	Crusting	Pickle
Pureeing	Making quenelle	Raw	Drying	Crispy-seared
Soufflé	Slice		Powder	Sous-vide
Making savory tartlets	Chiffonade		Smoke	
Shaped gels	Julienne		Fried fine julienne	
Tourner	Batonnet		Grilled	
Small dice, Brunoise	Steamed			
Gratinée	Poached			
Braised				
Roasted				

Each style brings previous styles' processes into a contemporary understanding—these are not exclusive listings. To see how this chart might be helpful, consider any ingredient and look at what processes might be used in working with that ingredient within the different styles. The point is not to force any ingredient into working with all the processes available but rather to understand how the arrived-at look of the ingredient creates flavor, which is part of a style's characteristics.

Choosing an ingredient and then executing all the culinary processes applicable to that ingredient can be thought of as an *ingredient extension*. An example of a carrot extension can be found in the color inset Image 28. Earlier styles within the *culinary Art history* would not have the same possibilities of cooking processes as later styles.

Consider the possibilities of an artichoke. In Classical, an artichoke might be stuffed with pork and mushroom duxelle to be braised; or, artichokes might be cooked, arranged in a circle, covered with cream sauce and parmesan cheese and gratined, topped with a truffle slice. Sliced artichoke bottoms might be cooked in cream sauce and served on top of a large crouton. Artichoke bottoms might be used to hold other vegetables such as peas or creamed asparagus tips to form a pyramid. Or, the bottoms might be filled with a cone of foie gras breaded and deep-fried (Escoffier 1982, 478).

FIGURE 11.1

The Possibilities of an Artichoke. This image, going from left to right, shows how an artichoke might be presented in Classical, Nouvelle, New American, and Global styles.

A Nouvelle chef is more likely to steam young artichokes and lightly dress them in butter to present halved or quarter. Or, the bottoms might be cooked and cut into slices that are fanned out in an arrangement. A Fusion style chef might make artichoke carpaccio or sushi roll, while in the New American style, artichokes might be cut in half and finished on the grill. Artichoke bottoms could be sliced and made into chips or cubed and used as a layer in a stack. In Global style, the artichokes might be expressed in a foam consistency or made into a savory sorbet, or baby leaves might be scattered in a deconstructed presentation.

GARNISH AND PLATE DESIGN

The way a chef thinks about garnishing a plate reveals, perhaps more than any other single factor, what her Professional style is. Is garnishing something added onto a plate, like a piece of jewelry is added to an outfit, or is garnishing a result of cooking processes and ingredients—in other words, the clothes of the outfit? The concept of garnishing has changed throughout the styles, reflecting changing ideas about design ornamentation. In French, the word *garnir* implies furnishing. In English, the word *garnish* evolved to reference appearance rather than utility ("Garnish" 2011).

FIGURE 11.2

Edible "Jewelry." An assortment of garnishes from the different Professional styles.

Around the same time as Escoffier first published *Le Guide Culinaire*, the decisive Classical work for U.S. chefs, art and design were entering the modern period. Modernism is a cultural phenomenon that encompasses ideas about breaking with tradition. Such artists were self-conscious about the processes they used to be creative, much as Techno-emotive chefs today are. They broke with traditional ways of organizing compositions and tried to let the materials speak through abstract forms. Modern designers eschewed all decorations added on to a design. There was to be no ornamentation in buildings and products; the materials themselves should be expressive. Global style, with its emphasis on the individual characteristics of ingredients, is the beginning of professional cuisine's modern period, but its interaction with a postmodern world allows for a mash-up of all previous styles.

Classical garnishes were actually the vegetable and starch accompaniments to animal proteins. They were what would now be referred to as side dishes. These accompaniments to central dishes were, compared to today's standards, elaborately constructed with geometric cuts and shaping of the ingredients. These were then placed in a regular pattern around the central food. Sauces were often garnished with precise cuts of such things as vegetables, truffles, and bone marrow. It was a modern approach to the extensive decoration of Table and Room presentations achieved by geometric placement of complex *dish* constructions.

Nouvelle chefs eschewed the complexity of these side dishes and chose instead to create ornamental looks through plating. Ingredients were not constructed into elaborate side dishes but, rather, each ingredient was cooked separately and placed in a symmetrical pattern on the plate. Plates could be further embellished by dotting and dragging of sauces within sauces. Garnishing was expressed as the addition of small sprigs of herbs, slices of fruit, or fried ingredients that decorated the plate. Thus, garnishing changed from being component dishes of the plate to being the addition of decorative foods that ornament the plate. Yet, the decorative embellishment of Nouvelle plates was more like pleasing patterns in clothes, fabrics with a good weave, or attractive buttons rather than jewelry.

Fusion and New American chefs continued to use add-on garnishes of fried ingredients and herbs but generally did not so rigidly pattern food or sauce placements. Height was often the embellishing touch to New American plates and stacks or mounds might be topped with a cloud of fried julienne vegetables. Dried vegetable powders or spices were sometimes used to draw lines or sprinkled on New American plates for added flavor and ornamentation. Fusion garnishing allowed for Japanese-style cuts of raw vegetables and also edible flowers to be used on hot plates. The idea of using a cold garnish that is more a piece of eye candy than appetizing foodstuff was a very different approach; these garnishes truly were more jewelry-like.

As plate construction began to replace the dish presentations—in other words, as chefs created flavors to fit a plate instead of plating created *dishes*—the concept of garnishing once again changed. The presentation method causes the food to be "adorned with a property or quality" that is itself beautiful ("Garnish" 2011). The way foods are plated had always been part of the look, but in Global style the plating was done in an abstract way to highlight the ingredients themselves without a clear reference to the unity of the *dish*.

Wasabi Extension. This image is an example of an ingredient extension; choosing any ingredient, the cook then proceeds to make various textures from it using different culinary processes. The image shows, from left to right, wasabi sauce made from powder, molded wasabi paste, and fresh, "real" wasabi root, grated.

Chefs have always considered how the finished dish will present as they prepare ingredients, but in Global style, the method of preparation was used to reflect a particular characteristic of an ingredient. Thus, Global plates' attractiveness is not achieved by choosing pieces of clothing or jewelry but rather by applying design techniques to everyday fabrics.

Consider, for example, how wasabi might be served on a sushi plate. On the one hand, if the wasabi is provided as a small dish of green sauce, it functions primarily as a condiment—flavor that can be added to the dish. Thus, it adds visual attractiveness primarily through its color. On the other hand, if the wasabi is presented as a molded paste, like a leaf, it functions first as a visual embellishment through shape and color. Finally, if the wasabi is grated from fresh root, then it becomes part of the plate construction—an element of the dish being created through plating. The texture and form function simultaneously, as visual impact and flavor components of the plate. The wasabi as condiment sauce is closest to how a Nouvelle chef approaches garnishing; the molded leaf wasabi is closer to a Classic idea of decorating, and the fresh grated wasabi is like a Global use of ingredients for embellishment.

THE PLATE ITSELF

Chefs in most instances work within the constraints of the serviceware available to them, but sometimes even those parameters are very wide. There might be a choice of different-sized round plates; there might be a number of different shapes such as triangles, rectangles, and squares; there might be different color options, like solid black or clear glass. There might be different forms, including standard flat serviceware and standard bowls, as well as newer styles of large rims with a small center circle and bowls with rims that extend out many inches from a small cup. There might be sectioned plates or small plates. It is in part fashion that guides the chef's choice of a certain type of serviceware, but her choice is also guided by what would be the best carrier to express flavor in a certain *dish*.

Almost all Classical, Nouvelle, and New American presentations were done on round plates. The size varied from approximately 9-inch to 12-inch rounds with defined rims. The rims were sometimes decorated with a simple color band or graphic patterns but were often plain white. The sauces fit in the round defined by the rim and were of enough thickness to hold a ring or circle shape. Stacks and Mound designs were sometimes served in a large soup plate or pasta plate that could contain the more broth-like sauces. In addition, small cups and glasses were sometimes used for the Trio designs—these would be placed on a dinner plate.

Later, compartmentalized rectangles and squares were used in Trio designs and also for Fusion presentations. Fusion style changed the way restaurants bought china. For Classical and Nouvelle restaurants, plates had to match throughout the entire service of the menu. Larger or smaller round plates of the same design were used to serve almost all courses. As Fusion and New American styles became more popular, restaurants often had different-shaped plates, and one diner might have a round plate while others at the same table might have square or rectangular plates. Whereas originally distinction was shown by an extensive collection of serviceware all of the same line, later, significance was demonstrated by the variety of serviceware used.

As presentations became more linear and deconstructed, rimmed plates were replaced by rimless rounds and squares. These matched the more textured sauces of Global designs, and Global presentations often rely on interplay between the physical characteristics of the serviceware and ingredients. For example, small cups surrounded by a large rim aid in the presentation of broth-like sauces with Mound designs elaborated with a foam.

Seeing a new piece of serviceware can inspire new ways of plating. A different color, shape, or form might change the types of ingredients that come to mind or cause reconsideration of the textures given to those ingredients. Like the question of the chicken and the egg, it is difficult to state which comes first for the plate and the presentation. The piece of serviceware used to serve *dishes* shapes the food literally as well as conceptually. The design of *dishes* necessitates certain characteristics of serviceware so that the *dishes* can be served and eaten at their best.

◎ SOUP AS AN EXAMPLE OF FUNDAMENTALS

Soup is an obvious example of using serviceware so that a food can be served and eaten at its best. By considering how soup is presented, some obvious facts about matching the presentation to the plate are exposed. If soup is served on a flat plate, the first thing that happens is that it cools off too quickly. So, in choosing a plate for a presentation, we know that the shape of the serviceware must help maintain the correct temperature of the food being served. For soup, a bowl is deeper and creates less exposed soup surface—thus, it stays hotter longer. Some soup bowls have lids to maintain even more heat, or sometimes soup is served tableside from a pitcher, which keeps the soup hot and also allows for the garnishing of the soup bowl. This was part of the reason that initially *dishes* were not plated in the kitchen. Instead, the *dishes* were assembled tableside by wait staff; vegetables, starches, sauces, and meats were more easily kept hot.

If the diner is expected to pick up the bowl and drink the soup instead of using a spoon, then choosing a soup bowl with two handles makes that easier for the customer. Drinking from a flatter bowl, like a soup plate, is much more difficult to do without spilling. Therefore, if a chef is presenting a trio of soups on a larger dinner plate, each of the small soup bowls is likely to have a handle. But if a chef is presenting a bowl of soup that has a garnish in it, it is more likely the soup will be presented in a flatter soup plate with a spoon. Most often soup is served in ceramic, not glass, serviceware because glass will transfer the heat more quickly. In a glass vessel, the soup loses more heat and the vessel may be unsafe for a customer to touch.

Serving soup in taller bowls makes it easier to move them from the kitchen to the dining room without spilling or dirtying the rim. This is also the reason why, when soup is presented in soup-plates rather than taller bowls, it is often ladled or poured tableside. Saucers are almost always served under all soup bowls, in case the customer has a slight spill, except for the newer style oversized bowls. These larger bowls are generally designed to work with mound or pedestal presentations, where the broth is functioning more as a sauce than a soup.

Consommé is generally served in a taller style soup bowl with handles on either side; these are often referred to as consommé cups. This was so that the diner could drink the broth and finish eating the garnish with a spoon. In general, the thinner the soup, the more likely the bowl is to be taller than flatter. Flatter soup plates work better for soups that have chunks in them or are thick enough for a spoon to scrape up the last of the *dish*.

In looking at the basic soup course, it should be evident that the way a customer is expected to eat the dish has a lot to do with what serviceware is best. It should also be evident that the presentation and its plate should maintain the desired qualities of the *dish*, such as hotness for soup. In addition, it should be noted that by changing the way the service staff work, the presentation can be enhanced, with soup poured table-side, or that if a dish is plated in the kitchen, it must be able to be carried into the dining room without affecting the presentation.

Soup may be attractive simply through its texture and color, or the precise knife cuts used in a clear soup may look pleasing and mix and fit on a spoon. Additional embellishment is sometimes desired, and chefs often achieve this by presenting tableside, choosing a more elaborate bowl, or presenting a trio of small bowls in a sampler plate. Another way of serving more than one soup at a time is to pour two different soups of a creamy thick consistency into two sides of the same bowl.

However, soups can be garnished beyond the intrinsic characteristics of preparation, service, and serviceware choice. Ingredients, or *dishes*, may be placed in the empty bowl, or placed on top of the soup, or accompanying foods may be served on the side. For example, it is traditional to serve a crisp embellishment on the side, such as crackers, an elongated bread crouton, a savory tuile, a puff pastry straw, or a vegetable chip.

If garnishes are to be placed on top of the soup, they should correspond with the ingredients in the soup; to place raw carrot julienne on top of clam chowder is simply bad jewelry. It does not convey to the diner anything about the soup, nor does it deepen or play counterpoint to the soup's flavor.

Sometimes a condiment is served on the side so that a diner may add as little or as much as they prefer. Boula-Boula, a green pea and green turtle soup that is no longer made due to the abuse of the worldwide turtle population, was embellished by serving a thimble-size glass of sherry and a small bowl of whipped cream on the side. The sherry

FIGURE 11.4

Various Styles of Soup Serviceware. In this image, different styles of soup plates, bowls, and cups are shown. The type of soup, number of courses, and price will influence the serviceware choice.

could be poured into the soup or drunk separately, and the whipped cream could be dolloped on top, to the delight of the diner. Of course, savory flavored whipped cream could be piped or quenelled on an appropriate soup in the kitchen, just as a seasoned oil or other liquid could be drawn as a swirl or placed carefully as drops on top of the soup.

Thus, from these examples of presentation variables for soup, the following universals can be constructed.

Guidelines that Apply to All Presentations

◆ The serviceware used to plate must maintain the integrity of the food, such as correct serving temperature.

◆ The serviceware used to plate must assure the ease of eating for the diner.

◆ The plating must be executed so that all ingredients and dishes remain at their optimal state, such as crispy items not getting soggy.

◆ The plating must facilitate transportation from the kitchen to the diner without upset.

◆ Although the eye might eat first, embellishments should always be edible and correspond to the other ingredients of the *dish* or plate.

◎ BACK TO THE MENU

Once all the decisions are made about ingredients, culinary processes, saucing, and serviceware, it is time to re-evaluate these decisions in the style of the menu. Each style has a different philosophy of how courses are sequenced in a menu and how these courses should relate to each other. Therefore, once a menu is written, all plating must be considered in light of the entire range of choices on the menu, especially in a chef's tasting menu or special event menu.

First, place the plate in the course sequence of the menu; then, examine the overall menu to see what food choices, culinary processes, or sauces were already applied or will be applied in the menu. Is repetition of these elements desired in this type of menu?

Examine the menu sequence to see if the consistency of an adjacent course is too similar; is creamy followed by creamy? Look at the serving temperatures for each course; do they fit the pattern of the menu's style? Also, examine closely how the flavors are to be experienced in the style's menu; does the new plate "play" right?

Example Using a Classical / Nouvelle Menu Sequence

Course	Temperature	Intensity of Spice / Flavor
Cold hors d'oeuvre	Cold	Light
Soup	Hot	Light, but richer
Fish	Hot	Medium
Sorbet	Cold	Sharp, clean
Meat	Hot	Heavier, rich
Salad	Cold	Sharp, clean
Cheese	Cold	Rich
Dessert	Hot/cold	Richest

The menu style clarifies whether the plating choices work overall in terms of the meal. Parameters concerning ingredient choices, culinary processes, saucing, and serviceware are shaped by the other courses in the menu, even if the menu is a mental abstraction for the type of meal this plate might be served in.

QUERIES & INQUIRIES

1. What causes a change in a Frame of *culinary Art history*?

2. What causes a style to change within a Frame of *culinary Art history*?

3. What are culinary processes?

4. After choosing a focus food for a plate, what questions develop?

5. What is garnishing for chefs working in the following styles: Classical, Nouvelle, Fusion, and Global?

6. What guidelines apply to all presentations?

7. In this inquiry you are to do a partial ingredient extension. Execute all the knife cuts you can think of on one vegetable; now list all the possible uses you can think of for each knife cut. For example, julienned zucchini might suggest:

   ◆ Sauté, steaming, fried for garnish, raw preparation such as salad, pickled, as a component of a crust

8. In this exercise you are to do a partial ingredient extension. Choose a different vegetable and list all the textures you could make with that vegetable. Here is an example using red bell pepper:

   ◆ Mince, brunoise, small dice, julienne, roast, bake, grill, barbeque, poach, fry, stew, sauté, puree, pickle, soufflé, juice, gel, foam, coulis, frothy emulsion, syrup, cloud, oil, custard, powder

9. Consider the three variables of plating—sauce, focus food, and culinary process. Create a Face plate using a focus food, such as chicken breast, with two side dishes, such as potatoes and carrots.

   a. Choose one of the two side dishes on the Face and change that side dish using a different culinary process.
      i. Does the plate taste the same?
      ii. Do you think it could be better presented now that one side dish is different?
      iii. Does this suggest changes to the other side dish or the focus food?
   b. Using the same original Face plate, leave the focus food and the two side dishes the same but change the texture or viscosity of the sauce.
      i. Does the plate taste the same?
      ii. Do you think it could be better presented now that the sauce is different?
      iii. Does this suggest changes to the side dishes or the focus food?
   c. Using the same original Face, re-plate the dishes into another arrangement; the most obvious is the BUFF.
      i. Does the plate taste the same?
      ii. Do you think you need to make changes to the textures to get the plate to work better in this different arrangement?

10. Create a Stack design of three layers where all the layers are composed of small, diced ingredients. Then create another stack of the same ingredients but change the order of the layers. After sampling both stacks, is there a difference in flavor?

11. Using the same ingredients, create another Stack where only two of the layers are made of small diced ingredients and the third layer is a different texture, such as a puree. Does this stack taste different from the original? Was it the same, easier, or harder to cut and eat?

12. This last exercise can be used to summarize all that you have learned up to this point, or it might be used to investigate a different area of Professional cuisine other than artistic dining.

If you choose to explore a different culinary context, use the parameters for menu research given in Chapter 2 and go as far back as possible to gather examples of foods served in that way. Examine if there are different presentation styles that would create Frames within the selected culinary context.

Either for artistic dining or in your chosen culinary context, investigate each style for foods valued, sources of inspiration, and garnishing techniques. Use the following table to summarize your understandings of the culinary focus area.

Culinary context / area of Professional cuisine (Defined by food category, price point, service style, & menu format)	Artistic dining	
Menu Frame: Period of Professional cuisine (This might not be applicable if you have a focus area such as snacks.)	Plate	Examples of responses for one style within the Plate Frame of artistic dining
Style within menu frame:	Nouvelle	
Archetypical (Plate) design patterns:	Sun, Fan, Island(s)	
Typical foods eaten or course sequence:		
Flavor emphasis in course sequence:		
Cooking processes used:		
Valued food elements:		
Sauces used:		
Garnishing techniques:		
Inspiration sources:		
Chefs, cookbooks representative of this style:		
Aesthetics valued:		
Effect of design on flavor:		

CITATION AND REFERENCE MATERIALS

Escoffier, Auguste. *Le Guide Culinaire*. Trans. H. L. Cracknell and R. J. Kaufmann. New York: Mayflower Books, 1982.

"garnish, v. (entries 4a,b,6)." OED Online (March 2011). Oxford University Press. Retrieved April 11, 2011, at www.oed.com/view/Entry/76840?rskey=54WjDC&result=2&isAdvanced=false.

Mariani, Jon F. *The Dictionary of American Food and Drink*. New York: William Morrow and Company, 1994, p. 38.

12

Critiquing Culinary Art

Critiques are part of a dialogue that fosters growth in the culinary community. They help to share and create knowledge about successful plating techniques. The goal of this chapter is to examine how information needs to be gathered for a critique to have meaning for all participants in the process.

WHEN: TIMES FOR CRITIQUING

Chefs and cooks are constantly receiving feedback about their food. It may be an immediate reaction from a co-worker or a diner, or it may be a more formalized assessment by a chef, supervisor, food writer, or culinary judge. Principally, there are six instances when presentation is explicitly discussed:

1. When a chef is assessing how closely a cook is matching the plated standard
2. When a cook, team of cooks, or chef is presenting a new dish to a deciding power for approval to sell
3. When a chef is evaluating a special created by a cook
4. When a restaurant critic is reviewing a restaurant or event
5. When a cook, team, or chef is participating in a culinary competition
6. When a culinary art instructor is evaluating a student's work

The goals of these critiques are similar in that they all seek to provide feedback about how a certain dish fulfills expectations, which leads to these questions:

◆ Why is the plate being assessed?

◆ Who is doing the assessment?

◆ What are the expectations that are being assessed?

◆ How do underlying theories of food influence the assessment?

◎ WHY: REASONS FOR CRITIQUING

When a plate is being evaluated, the cook or chef who created the plate often feels that she, herself, is being evaluated and, in part this is true. The professional self of that cook or chef is being evaluated, not her intrinsic worth as a human being. If the person doing the evaluation is doing so in an effort to improve the cook or chef, or the overall standards of an operation or the culinary profession, then the method and language of the evaluation should reflect that underlying reason. The most important reason for any culinary critique is to increase knowledge.

This is why I have chosen to use the word *critique* rather than *criticism*, although both words are listed as synonymous in dictionaries. Both words describe the act of judging, but criticizing has a negative connotation, leaving little hope for improvement, while critiquing suggests judgments that lead to a fuller understanding and analysis. The important point is not if the evaluation is called a criticism or critique but rather that the reason for the assessment in all cases should be positive—positive in the sense that it gives a language to food experiences that furthers the development of an individual and, subsequently, the culinary community.

Why critiques are done always relates to the context of where they are done. When a chef is assessing how closely a plate matches the plated standard of a menu, the reason for this type of evaluation is straightforward; the customer's expectations for a menu description need to be matched by the plate, and all platings that are served when that menu item is ordered should be the same.

The reasons for the other five instances are not as uncomplicated because they relate to expectations and theories that might not be clearly stated. For instance, sometimes when plates are critiqued, there is disagreement between the chef or cook that created the plate and the judging panel or person, or even among the judging panel members. These disagreements usually arise because the criteria used to evaluate the plate are not explicitly clear, or an assumption is made that all of the chefs, cooks, and evaluators share a common understanding of what food should be like. Who is giving a critique is as important as what criteria are used to judge a plate.

◎ WHO: THE HUMAN FACTOR

There is a long tradition of considered thought, criticism, relating to art works. For craft works, there is not as much of an established dialogue, which arises from the fact that until recently, purposeful objects were not considered to hold aesthetic value. Although there is much writing related to food, it has not coalesced into a formalized system; instead, most culinary writing relates the food to a personal experience that does not correspond to generalities of critical knowledge. In other words, food writing is often expressed as, "I like it," or, "It's not good, I don't like it." These sensual evaluations are what scholars see as the stumbling block to considering food in an objective or aesthetic way. For instance, to comment that a dish tastes "good" is hard to measure, but to state that the knife cuts of a dish are technically correct is easily measured by anyone. Thus, food is often incorrectly believed to be too personal, too corporeal to be considered with the necessary formal distance.

Yet, when a chef makes an evaluation of a plate, there are criteria being used beyond personal preferences that relate to a shared understanding of practice in Professional cuisine. As an example, here is a short list of criteria often considered by chefs during a critique:

Is the seasoning level appropriate?

Are the flavors balanced on the plate?

Is an appropriate amount of sauce provided?

Are the textures varied on the plate?

Are the foods cooked correctly?

Does the presentation go out onto the rim of the plate?

The criteria that were developed for each of the styles in Chapters 4 to 7 reflect the necessity of evaluating plates within the changing standards of the different styles: Classical, Nouvelle, New American, Fusion, and Global. Additional criteria used by chefs are discussed in the next section.

For anyone to give a meaningful assessment of food, there needs to be a critical language to articulate the analysis, coupled with reflective practice. Experience alone is not enough to create an expert, although it is fundamental; the know-how has to be thought about.

The Chef Evaluator

A chef is an expert who has spent tens of years honing and perfecting technical ability and building a successful practice. To do this, the chef has had to consider how to build menus and please customers. The chef has also had to develop a management style that allows her to get the best out of her cooks by recognizing what they need to be their best. To be a chef, you must first have mastery over techniques and methods and know when to use and apply that knowledge. For example, the chef in a restaurant can step into *each and every* station on the line and perform as well as, if not better than, the line cook. This is where her authority comes from. To criticize what you cannot do yourself is bogus; to not accept criticism from an accomplished chef is immature. Trust is at the heart of all successful endeavors, and a cook must trust the chef like a climber trusts the lead mountaineer.

If you are working in foodservice for a reason beyond the money, then you are striving for some sort of growth and satisfaction. When you go to a culinary school or work for a chef, in essence, what you are affirming is that by following their lead, you will grow and hopefully one day lead in turn. This growth builds into new understandings and directional changes in styles. Oftentimes, beginning cooks will state, "Well, *I* like it," when criticism is given, but this statement holds three pitfalls:

1. You are reverting to a personal, and amateurish, statement of preferences that denies your participation within a professional tradition. You are using what I call the YUM–YUK scale.

2. You are denying the learning that experiences brings; thus, in a way, you are saying that you cannot improve because whatever you do is fine already.

3. You are not developing a professional eye because you are refusing to see outside of your own personal viewpoint.

Even though chefs might disagree when they are evaluating food, for example, during a competition, there still exists a commonality of evaluative practices. Sometimes the disagreements are based in quantitative assignments—this one is best; this one is second best. Often these disagreements are based in differences of styles. For example, an evaluating chef whose style is firmly based in New American might not see the value of a deconstructed plate in the Global style. The food might be too abstracted from its natural state for a chef who prefers a BUFF presentation. That is a large part of the reason why it is so important to understand the various styles that exist within Professional cuisine. It is then possible to articulate the style from which you judge, and you, in turn, can more easily understand the style differences of others.

Contrasting Styles. This image shows two BLTs. The choice of ingredients remains the same, as does the food cost, but the style of presentation is different. Does it change your perceived value of the BLTs? Do you think one presentation would taste better than the other?

The Food Critic

Restaurant critics often come from diverse traditions outside the hospitality industry; in this way, they are evaluating as an informed consumer. Our customers' opinions are very important, as they represent the bottom line. Without customers, you are not a professional cook but a skilled amateur. Just as the public is a necessary part of critical success, so, too, are the critics because under the best circumstances they increase public knowledge about our work. Also, they have defined trends in our work, which then generates further growth and understanding in our field.

For example, one of the factors that gave rise to the dominance of French cuisine as the model for many professional standards was the importance that French culture placed on food. This significance was, in part, created and developed by French gastronomes. Alexandre Balthazar Laurent Grimod de La Reynière, often simply referred to as Grimod, is considered by some as the first restaurant critic. He was a contemporary of the famous gastronome Jean Anthelme Brillat-Savarin; both produced important culinary writings during the first quarter of the nineteenth century. Their writings articulated what a good meal should be and how it is best appreciated. This not only created culinary theories but also helped spread the dominance of those culinary theories.

Gastronomy is the field of knowledge centered on eating. It is an umbrella term that combines food understandings through many disciplines such as history, science, aesthetics, and physiology. The word implies considered eating, refinement—not simply consumption.

A **gourmet** is a connoisseur; such a person develops their palate to be sensitive to the subtleties of food and drink. Connoisseurs are considered to be experts in matters of taste as a result of their extensive knowledge.

A **gastronome** is a person much like a gourmet, or connoisseur, who cultivates understanding about food and drink but also goes on to write about her opinions.

Restaurant reviews encourage interest and help to create an informed customer base. Yet, the expertise of the restaurant critic is rarely considered. The reasons for their pronouncements, beyond personal preferences, are often not clear. Expertise, itself, has become suspect in recent times. The scandal that centered on the suicide of a three-star chef and the Michelin guide raised many questions about the legitimacy of rating restaurants. But a critical discourse is necessary for an art/craft form to be fully appreciated and further developed. So then, who is best situated to critique food? Is it simply a matter of popularity or personal preference? The answer to such questions depends on focus. If the focus of the critic is to simply inform other diners of the preferences of someone like themselves, then popularity votes, like the ones found in the Zagat guides, are helpful. But if the focus is the growth and development of the culinary community, then there must be some expertise behind the evaluations that comes from and leads to critical thinking.

◎ WHAT: ELEMENTS OF A CRITIQUE

For any critique to be successful there must be understanding about what is being evaluated; this relates to the context of the evaluation. If a cook or chef is presenting a new special or a new menu item for acceptance, then the first considerations are based on the existing menu. If a cook or chef is presenting a plate in a competition or in a kitchen class, then the first considerations for success are based on some type of scoring sheet, which, if properly developed, takes the place of a successful menu.

The first part of a critique should evaluate how well a plate fits the culinary context; there are two other areas of considerations in a critique: technical execution and design. At the end of this chapter, there is sample evaluation that brings these three areas of a critique together.

Culinary Context

Critiques should always be situated within a culinary context: food category, price point, service style, and menu format. The following are the types of questions that should begin a food critique:

Does the plate match the defined food category?

For example, if a sandwich is being presented and the defined food category is breakfast, is it a breakfast sandwich?

Do the ingredients reflect the price point of the food?

A breakfast sandwich served at an upscale hotel might have truffle shavings on it, but such shavings would be prohibitive in a value menu sandwich.

Does the food presentation fit the method of service that will be used to deliver the food?

For example, if a sandwich is plated, is there enough empty space at the edges of the plate for the plate to be easily moved without the food being disturbed?

Does the presented food fit into a course or category of the defined menu format?

A breakfast sandwich might fit an à la carte breakfast menu with multiple categories such as eggs and potatoes, pancakes and waffles, or burritos and sandwiches, but it might not be appropriate on a special events menu as an opening course, coming before an egg dish served with toast.

This poses problems in competitions where chefs are asked to create one dish, because sometimes even though no menu concept is given, there exist hazy concepts of what the menu might be in the mind of a judge. So, when creating a plate for a competition, it is useful to imagine a menu even if it is not part of the typical competition scoring sheet because it causes you to think more clearly and deeply about the choices you make. For example, here is a typical scoring sheet for plated presentations:

FIGURE 12.2

That Looks Expensive. In this image, the same steak-cut is presented in two different ways. Could you charge more money for the steak presented on the plate compared to the steak presented in the basket?

Criteria	Maximum Possible Points	Points Awarded	Comments
Serving method & presentation	10		
Portion size / nutritional balance	15		
Ingredient compatibility	5		
Cooking skills / culinary technique	10		
Taste: flavor / texture / doneness	25		
Creativity	10		
Total	75		

(Leonard 2006, 119)

The problem of relying on this type of evaluation is that when using it, judges rely on almost subconscious evaluative standards relating to their preferred style of Professional cuisine. In other words, they are judging a plate based on hypothetical menus and customers from their previous experiences. If Professional style is not one of the first categories of a scoring sheet, then all participants are making their own assumptions about what defines success.

Adding to the confusion brought about by unarticulated assumptions concerning Professional styles are less than specific point scales. If a category is worth 25 points, then ideally there would be 25 criteria that either are or are not achieved in the presentation. This type of exactitude in specifics levels the assessment but also removes the expertise of the evaluator and ignores the combined effect the parts play in creating the whole.

One possible method to correct this type of confusion is to relate numeric scales to possible responses of hypothetical customers; this would also ensure that the evaluation reflects standards that would also be successful in a professional kitchen. For instance, in evaluating a Hollandaise sauce, most chefs tasting the same Hollandaise will agree if it is good or not, but it is very difficult to list the criteria of a good Hollandaise and weight the points for each criteria so that the result reflects the practice of working kitchens. The efforts to list criteria of a good Hollandaise within a rubric can easily lead to a sauce that would not be acceptable in a restaurant being passable in a grading context. Instead, consider the following, more holistic, numeric scale:

5	The customer can be expected to suggest eating at this restaurant to others. The customer would return to the restaurant and order this exact dish again.
4	The customer can be expected to return to the restaurant but not talk about it to others.
3	The customer might return to the restaurant but will not order this exact dish again.
2	The customer will not be happy to pay for this experience. The customer will tell other people not to waste their time and money.
1	The customer refuses to pay for such poor food.
0	The customer leaves without receiving food.
−5	The customer gets sick.

Numbers have a way of simplifying synergies, which can be misleading. **The whole of any food presentation is, ultimately, greater than the sum of its parts**. So, when evaluating food, it is always best to do so in relation to the hypothetical customer or an existing menu.

Technical Execution

This is the area of a critique where most chefs see food exactly the same way: the technical executions of preparing food. The evaluation of these skills is also often rated on a numerical scale, such "Proper Cooking Techniques" or "Knife Cuts" 1–10. This is again misleading because in a working kitchen, these criteria are more like on or off switches: this is right or this is wrong. For example, if you are executing a braise on meat and the result is slightly stringy, it is really not right, but to take into consideration the experience level of the cook and the synergy of the braise with other items on the plate, scoring is done in shades of correctness.

Assuming that all cooks and chefs share the same culinary background and traditions creates difficulties; judging or executing a *dish* or culinary process without having previous experience with it does not permit development of the understanding necessary for a fair evaluation or a successful presentation. In this regard, for cooks and chefs, it is as important to have eating experiences as it is to have cooking experience. Consider this recommendation to be eating assignments. As much as is possible within your budget, you should go to sources of excellent eating so that when you incorporate a method or technique in your cooking, you have already experienced an expert's rendition of it. For instance, if you would like to develop a very stylized plate that has a barbequed meat as a focus, you should first eat barbeque in as many great barbeque houses as possible before adapting the technique.

Technical ability begins with the proper handling of ingredients. For example, mashed potatoes seem like such a simple dish to prepare, but it is often the simplest of dishes that are in truth the most difficult. First, the right type of potatoes must be chosen, and they need to be stored correctly to retain their goodness. Then, the potatoes must be peeled correctly so as to not leave any taste of earth or greenness from the skin. Next, the potatoes must be boiled so that they become soft, not underdone or overdone. After that, the cooked potatoes should not be shocked, like some other vegetables, but spread on a sheet pan and lightly dried in the oven. Finally, the dried potatoes are then riced and beaten with hot milk and butter. If the potatoes are run in a food processor instead of being beaten, they will become waxy and the texture will also lack airiness. Every taste during an evaluation exposes these types of preparation choices, and these choices can usually be seen by an experienced eye before tasting even begins.

Thus, the beginning of evaluations in the area of technical ability should begin with scoring categories such as:

◆ The ingredients were handled properly.

◆ The ingredients were at the peak of their natural goodness.

◆ The ingredients were properly cleaned or trimmed.

◆ The knife skills match exactly among the cuts and to the standard of the cutting technique.

FIGURE 12.3

Presentation and Menu Placement. In this image, there are two presentations of fruit salad. On the left is a mixed fruit cup. The right-side presentation uses the same type and amount of fruit but is presented on a plate. Could these presentations be used interchangeably? Would they both be placed on a menu in the same place?

◆ The ingredients match the cooking techniques applied to them.

◆ The ingredients were cooked to the perfection of the method applied.

◆ The presentation is served at the correct temperature.

These are criteria of technical ability. Standards can be further developed for each type of cooking process, but hyper-developed specific criteria should be avoided. It is important to remember that ours is a craft-based profession, and respect for the chef's role in passing along information based on experience to younger cooks is critical in retaining our professional community. Putting all the details of achieving a successful execution of a cooking process into a list often loses the synergy of those details that truly makes it successful.

The result of all these judgments can be summed up into an often-heard phrase: *It's clean work*. This is a difficult phrase to explain but an easy condition to see. It has to do with being able to see the effort applied to ingredients; if the effort shows, the plate is not "clean." It relates to the ability of a cook to make difficult hand skills look easy— flawless. This means that there are no ragged edges in the details of any executions or in the combinations of executions on the plate.

Design

Design on a plate happens on two levels. The first consideration level is flavor and the second is presentation. Although this book is principally concerned with plate presentations, it is not possible to consider the look of food without considering its flavor as part of the design; if the look was considered without thinking about flavor, then the considerations would not be about actual food.

A good question to begin design evaluations is, "What is the visual focus of the plate?"

In some plate designs, such as the Deconstructed or Trio, there might be foci, but the subsequent question remains the same: Does the visual focus of the plate match the flavor being highlighted by the plate's written description?

If the answer is no, then why was such visual emphasis given to that element? There might be good reasons, but they need to be considered, because oftentimes, it is simply a design error.

Determining what flavors the diner is expected to perceive should be evident in the menu description and on the plate. Then, if any garnishes are used, it is more obvious to the evaluator if the garnish adds or detracts from the larger goal of expressing such stated flavors. A simple but effective question is, "Does the plate of food look better than it tastes?"

After having completed the many exercises in this book exploring the design of plates, the next question that should be asked is, "Could the flavors be better highlighted through a different design?" This is a distinct possibility; sometimes, in overcomplicating a design through too elaborate a culinary process, the flavor is lost in the look. Conversely, sometimes a plate design can be made more interesting by altering a culinary process to something slightly more complex. Thus, at this point in the evaluation, considerations are about how much complexity is necessary to express flavor. Increasing design complexity relates to serviceability, so the following questions should then be asked:

◆ Can the plate be reproduced in the necessary time by the kitchen staff within this service style?

◆ Can the plate be delivered to the diner without disruption of design or service?

◆ Will the diner have any problems eating this design?

Ultimately, good design is about asking the right set of questions. These questions differ in approach from evaluations of plates that stress the balancing and contrasting of design elements such as food selection, color, shape, texture, and cooking method. Rather, this type of evaluation suggests that design should begin by defining a culinary context. Within that context, the way the menu description is written suggests a Professional style that contains theories concerning food choices, culinary processes, and flavor expression. The actual language used to describe menu items creates expectations for the customers about values and presentation. Within these parameters plates are better evaluated.

◎ HOW: THEORIES INFLUENCE JUDGMENTS

When someone is evaluating a plate, all the beliefs they have about food influence their judgments. There were fewer differences of opinions when there was one dominant style in professional cooking, such as Classical style. Now, there are multiple styles where what is acceptable in one style breaks rules in another. Plurality in styles has been an issue for other areas of arts and crafts; without a tradition or an ideal that is agreed upon, it is difficult to avoid confusion.

The recognition of different styles within Professional cuisine aids in constructing a critical language that exposes theories behind design choices. The styles, and thus the archetypal plate designs, focus on different methods of expressing flavor. How a chef expresses flavor is based in two broad theoretical areas that set styles apart:

◆ The first set of ideas and beliefs centers on creativity.

◆ The second set of ideas and beliefs centers on flavor.

Creativity

Creativity is often a category in plating evaluations; all chefs agree that our profession advances through innovation. But, if innovation is done simply for the sake of originality, is that reason enough to do it? This question is answered by chefs based on their beliefs about what a dining experience should be and what a chef believes that diners look for when they make choices about dining. Thus, creativity is always assessed in relation to a hypothetical diner and a menu.

Creativity must make sense within some set of parameters. Chef James Peterson, in his book, *Sauces*, wrote, "If no one particular cooking tradition dominates, the diner as well as the cook becomes weary and confused. A fine meal should follow a single tradition and aesthetic—evoke a history, a place, and a people—not serve as an experimental testing ground for bizarre juxtaposition of flavors and styles" (Peterson 1998, 499).

Since the time of Escoffier, the need to innovate has been a driving market force. Novelty attracts attention, and innovation in design sells. However, the degree of how much innovation in comparison to how much imitation is where chefs differ.

Part of the answer is to be found in the background of our profession. Culinary art as a craft tradition has working methods that draw from art, science, and business; the area emphasized in a chef's practice will determine how much importance is placed on creativity. If a chef considers herself to be more an artist than an artisan, then innovation happens for its own sake, but for artisans, the innovation must first increase the value of the materials from nature, and the innovation must serve a purpose, such as more clearly expressing flavor. Consequently, chefs' evaluations of plating relate to their areas of emphasis within culinary art and also to their working theories about menus and customers.

Flavor

Ultimately, the goal of most culinary creativity is centered on flavor perception. Viewpoints about how flavor should be expressed form a continuum, where one end is occupied by chefs who believe a flavor that is associated with an ingredient should play clearly

Tomato – Garlic – Basil	......................................Tomato Sauce
Independent	New
Flavor	Flavor
Notes	Created

and independently from other elements on the same plate or in the *dish;* the other end of the flavor scale is occupied by chefs who believe that ingredients should be combined through culinary processes so that none of the original flavors are perceivable, but rather a new universal flavor is created.

In practice, chefs move along the flavor scale when making different menus or dishes. Sometimes flavors should blend; other times flavors should contrast, or be perceived independently. Plating creates flavor by causing the customer to eat the ingredients in different patterns, and the archetypal plate designs are achieved by changing shapes, textures, and placement of ingredients to affect these eating patterns.

The ways we think about presenting foods are expressions of our beliefs. Food on a plate is sending visual messages about culture and cuisine and about pervious chefs' work. The forms that food is presented in are symbols that express a practitioner's unspoken language. These forms and patterns of Professional cuisine are a visual language, which is rooted in historical developments. All culinary work relates to previous culinary work: Each chef's work is influenced by the work of other chefs and, in turn, influences the work of other chefs (Barrett 2000, 119).

Certain styles emphasize creativity more than others, and all the styles have different methods for creating flavor. Thus, when plate patterns are recognized as participating in a certain style of Professional cuisine, judging the success of presentations becomes less ambiguous and more contextually based. Critiques, then, are best when they not only describe what is actually being perceived on the plate but also associate these observations with professional traditions and theories.

Sample Critique Form

Point Scale: 0 = not achieved
                1 = effort presented
                2 = effort achieves satisfactory result
                3 = effort achieves good result			

List reason for critique:			
List acceptable Professional Styles:			
Has the food been produced in a safe / sanitary manner?		No **Stop**	Yes Continue

Culinary Context	Food Category	Service Style	Price Point
Culinary Context List intended parameters			
Does the plate match the defined food category?		No **Stop**	Yes Continue 1 2 3
Do the ingredients reflect the price point of the food?		0 1 2 3	
Does the food presentation fit the method of service that will be used to deliver the food?		No **Stop**	Yes Continue 1 2 3

Does the presentation match the needs of that service style?	
◆ Can the plate be reproduced in the necessary time within this service style?	0 1 2 3
◆ Can the plate be delivered to the diner without disruption of design or service?	0 1 2 3
◆ Will the diner have any problems eating this design?	0 1 2 3
List what course or category of the intended menu format the presentation is designed to fit.	
List where the planned placement of this plate is within the structure of the intended course sequence.	
◆ Is the serving size appropriate to the menu course?	0 1 2 3
◆ Are the flavorings, textures, temperature of the dish conducive to eating more food after this plate?	0 1 2 3

Technical Criteria	
The ingredients were handled properly.	0 1 2 3
The ingredients selected were at the peak of their natural goodness.	0 1 2 3
The ingredients were properly cleaned or trimmed.	0 1 2 3
The knife skills match exactly among the cuts and to the standard of the cutting technique.	0 1 2 3
The ingredients match the cooking techniques applied to them.	0 1 2 3
The ingredients were cooked/ processed to the perfection of the method applied.	0 1 2 3
The dish is appropriately seasoned.	0 1 2 3
The foods are served at the correct temperature.	0 1 2 3
Design	
Does the design of the plate correspond to the acceptable Professional styles?	0 1 2 3
Is the design visually balanced?	0 1 2 3
Are lines cleanly executed?	0 1 2 3
Is there sufficient unity between the elements of the plate?	0 1 2 3
Is there enough empty space for the plate to be "read" well?	0 1 2 3
Are the plate elements in proportion to each other and the serviceware?	0 1 2 3

Does the complexity or degree of difficulty in technical execution enhance the design?	0 1 2 3
Has creativity been demonstrated in meeting the requirements of the design?	0 1 2 3
List the focus food of the plate.	
Is the focus food clearly perceived?	0 1 2 3
Is the sauce appropriate to the plate & course placement?	0 1 2 3
If any garnishes are used, do they aid in perceiving flavor?	0 1 2 3
Do all foods and their seasoning work together to express this dish's flavor?	0 1 2 3
List what flavors the diner is expected to perceive.	
Is this level of flavor right for the menu placement?	0 1 2 3
Is the design balanced for flavor?	0 1 2 3
Does the presentation achieve the desired results of flavor through the use of temperature and texture?	0 1 2 3
Does the serviceware aid in maintaining the integrity of the food?	0 1 2 3
Do the colors aid the perception of desired flavor?	0 1 2 3
Total Points out of 99 possible	
Comments:	
◆ Could better flavor perception be achieved with a different plate arrangement?	
◆ Could better flavor perception be achieved with a different style of serviceware?	

QUERIES & INQUIRIES

1. In this chapter, what is the principal reason given for critiquing? Do your personal experiences of being evaluated support this understanding?

2. When are presentation critiques done?

3. Why are statements such as "I like the plate" not useful in a professional evaluation of a presentation?

4. What are the elements of a professional critique?

5. Who often gives critiques of presentations? Do these different types of people have different reasons for evaluating food? Does this change their focus and thus what they evaluate?

6. Investigate your own beliefs about plating:

   Culinary art will always be moored in some fundamental practices that must be respected in order to serve food. So, while there is a pluralism of styles, there still exists a consensus about fundamentals that validates all successful food. Technical mastery and skilled application of knowledge are at the core of this understanding. For instance, chefs might disagree about styles and expressions of flavor, but all chefs would agree that the first consideration of all food preparation is safety and sanitation.

   The following is a list of guidelines often suggested for plate presentations. It does not consider different styles but, rather, is a generalized list. As you read these guidelines, consider if they are true within all the styles and if all the archetypal plate designs would meet such criteria.

   Next to each guideline, note the style or styles in which it would be considered true. If you think that any guideline is true for all the styles of Professional cuisine, write ALL.

   ◆ Balance flavors on a plate; do not match extremely like flavors or unlike flavors. For example, do not mix creamy with creamy nor creamy with sour.

   ◆ Create a balance in flavors by pairing like cooking methods. For example, moist-heat cooked focus foods should be paired with moist-heat cooked side dishes while dry-heat cooked focus foods should be paired with dry-heat cooked side dishes.

   ◆ Do not over season. Highly seasoning many components of a dish or extremely seasoning one element of a dish will cause the flavors to be unperceivable.

   ◆ Use the appropriate amount of sauce; there should be enough for every bite of the food it accompanies. Do not put so little sauce on the plate that it is only a visual element of the presentation.

   ◆ Do not put too much sauce on the plate, causing foods to be masked by or swimming in it.

◆ Place the sauce to create an attractive pattern and also so that the cooking method of the accompanying food is not compromised. For instance, foods that have been browned should not be covered with sauce, which will dampen the caramelization.

◆ Use the natural colors of foods; use culinary processes that protect the natural colors but still provide the appropriate texture of ingredients.

◆ Do not use so many different colors that the plate looks gaudy; do not use so few colors that the plate looks bland.

◆ Vary the shape of the ingredients or *dishes* on a plate by choosing different natural shapes, by using knife cuts, or possibly by shaping. For example, presenting only stuffed vegetables or only small diced vegetables will not highlight the goodness of any of the vegetables.

◆ Vary the textures on a plate. Putting all smooth without any chunky or crispy will bore the mouth.

◆ Cook foods correctly so that the visual signals of a properly executed method are apparent. For instance, fried foods should look crispy, sautéed proteins should look browned.

◆ Serve hot food hot and cold food cold.

◆ Do not put hot and cold items on the same plate if the temperature of one will debase the texture of the other.

◆ Do not add an ingredient to a plate simply for its color.

◆ Do not add an item that will generally not be eaten such as a whole sprig of rosemary, citrus slice with rind, or a vegetable cup.

◆ Choose a plate that matches the appropriate serving portion; do not over-crowd a plate.

◆ Do not place food on the rim of the plate. Place the most attractive side of the food toward the diner.

◆ Do not spread food out so that it seems unrelated or unbalanced on the plate.

7. Consider the listed tenets / guidelines at the end of Chapters 4, 5, 6, 7, and also the guidelines that apply to all presentations in Chapter 11, as well as the criteria concerning technical ability (in this chapter) and the above list. Decide which tenets and guidelines describe your beliefs about plate presentation and create a list. Consider your style; is it strongly associated with any one of the established styles?

CITATION AND REFERENCE MATERIALS

Barrett, Terry. *Criticizing Art: Understanding the Contemporary*, 2nd ed. New York: McGraw-Hill Higher Education, 2000.

Chesser, Jerald W. *The Art and Science of Culinary Preparation*. Florida: The Educational Institute of the American Culinary Federation, 1992.

De Santis, Ronald. "B.U.F.F.-Up on Food Presentation." *The National Culinary Review* (Feb. 1998): 6–10.

Gablik, Suzi. *Has Modernism Failed?* New York: Thames and Hudson, 1984.

Keogh, Keith, and Culinary Team USA. *New Currents in American Cuisine*. Illinois: Cahners Publishing Company, 1993, pp. 250–251.

Keogh, Keith. "The Art of Plate Presentation." *The National Culinary Review* (Sept. 1999): 30–34.

Leonard, Edward G. *American Culinary Federation's Guide to Culinary Competitions; Cooking to Win!* Hoboken, NJ: John Wiley & Sons, Inc., 2006.

Mennell, Stephen. *All Manners of Food*, 2nd ed. Chicago: University of Illinois Press, 1996.

Peterson, James. *Sauces*, 2nd ed. New York: Van Nostrand Reinhold, 1998.

13

Culinary Values

How food is presented has always been important, to various degrees, whenever food is being served. Sayings such as, "The eye eats first," or, "My eyes were bigger than my stomach," demonstrate the role the look of food has on appetite. The look of food is also part of its marketing and reason for the media's attraction. Presentations sell food; they justify higher prices by increasing the customer's perceived value. While a poor presentation of good tasting food does lower its perceived value, a great presentation of poorly cooked or seasoned food achieves nothing.

This book began with the question, "Do you see what I mean?" The goal throughout the book has been to shift sight from a simple surface view to a deeper, substance view of plate presentations. The focus of the sight shift has been flavor. Yet, as complex as understanding how form and pattern create flavor is, this understanding is only part of the significance of plated presentations. The meanings of a plate presentation are multilayered and relate not only to what a chef is looking at on a plate but also to what a customer is looking for on a plate.

◎ WHAT IS VALUED BY CUSTOMERS

To say that something has value is to say that it is important. Food service operations are categorized based on the values they embrace, and customers chose different establishments based on what they value. The most basic factor relating to value is an economic one—inexpensive or expensive.

To say that you want to eat inexpensively does not mean that you want to eat poorly, which leads to the larger question of what it means to eat poorly. If someone eats poorly, does that mean that she does not eat enough food? Or, does that mean that she does not eat foods that promote health? Or, does that mean that she eats indiscriminately, paying no attention to the resources she is consuming? Or, does it mean that she eats food that is poorly prepared?

When chefs look at a plate of food, they can judge if it is "poor" in each sense of the word; they see layered meanings. Thus, when looking at a plated presentation, a chef can see in the quantity and choice of foods economic, nutritional, ecological, technical, and methodological values layered in with flavor and aesthetics.

Eating Well. Thanks to the resources available to many Americans, people can choose what and how much they would like to eat. This image shows a hypothetical plate made by a customer at a buffet. In what sense is this customer eating well?

The customers, by contrast, rarely have such a broad viewpoint. A customer purchasing food is looking for "something" which, in a general sense, can be labeled "good food." The meaning of "good" is relative to the needs, values, and desires of the customer in a specific instance. So, for one eating experience, "good" might be a hot plate piled with noodles, while on another occasion "good" might be a stacked tuna tartare.

To understand what "good" might mean to customers, you need to consider why people choose to eat away from home or purchase ready-made take out. A hungry person might be seeking satiation. In addition to hunger, though, a person might need nourishment; this differs in a degree of refinement from satiation in that it implies the customer is not simply looking to fill up but also to eat food that promotes some degree of health. A person might eat out or order takeout for the sake of convenience. A person might dine out to participate in a social situation or to celebrate an event. A customer may also choose to dine at an establishment to explore a food tradition or a chef's style. Thus, we can generalize six reasons a person may eat away from home or order takeout:

◆ Satiation

◆ Nourishment

◆ Convenience

◆ Sociability

◆ Celebration

◆ Exploration

Of course, there may be some combination of reasons, such as a person who goes out to eat because he is meeting friends to try a new restaurant, and who is also hungry. Food service operations exist to satisfy each of these needs and desires in different combinations at different price levels. Another issue that customers keep in mind, beyond basic motivation and price point, can be termed ethical considerations. These concerns might center on

FIGURE 13.2

Is this to go? Looking at this image of a presentation, which of the customer values do you think it is trying to satisfy? How could you change the presentation to make it satisfy different needs?

religious dietary restrictions, personal choices like vegetarianism, or ecological beliefs about sourcing foods. Thus, there are eight factor areas that can be defined as **customers' values**:

1. Price

2. Satiation

3. Nourishment

4. Convenience

5. Sociability

6. Celebration

7. Exploration

8. Ethical considerations

Although it might be easier to think about these values in a hierarchy of customers' needs and desires, that would not be accurate. These values are not mutually exclusive of each other or of specific types of food service; rather, an emphasis on any one value, or combination of values, is what defines different categories of establishments. It would also be a mistake to consider the customers' needs and values as hierarchical, as represented in the first pyramid.

The reality of a diner's concerns can take any order, once the base of hunger is fulfilled. The second pyramid represents such a possibility.

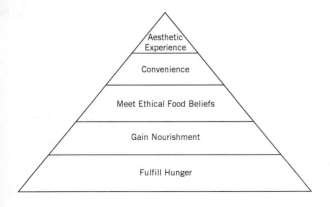

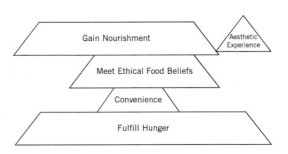

⦾ HOW A CHEF RELATES TO CUSTOMERS' VALUES

When a chef develops a menu, all these primary areas of concern need to be considered—not so that each need or desire can be meet, but rather to define a focus on what the establishment can do well. The menu is developed to provide value for a customer within a certain price range, so the chef is answering the question, "What do my customers value?" Using the list of customer values, a chef will create menus that fit the customers' needs by supplying the following:

Satiation		Large portions
Nourishment		Lower-fat and nutrient-dense foods
Convenience		Fast service
Sociability	with	Accommodating dining room layout
Celebration		Special event menus or Artistic dining
Exploration		Specialty food or Artistic dining
Ethical considerations		Locally sourced food; restricted animal proteins; sustainably raised or harvested

At this point, the chef's solutions to the anticipated customers' values revolve around the choice of foods offered, the price range, and the type of service; from these decisions, the chef will begin to think about culinary processes and presentation style.

If the establishment is going to offer plated table service, then the plate designs need to again match the anticipated customers' expectations. For example, fast service does not allow for complex presentations, and the customer looking for convenience is not generally focusing intently on details. Or, a customer whose main preoccupation is to fill up will not be pleased if the presentation sacrifices volume to achieve a certain look. It is artistic dining that emphasizes look as an integral part of flavor because the anticipated diner is seeking something more than satiation, nourishment, or convenience.

FIGURE 13.3

Multiple Meanings.
A food presentation does not simply meet customers' needs in one way. The food might meet several criteria for the customer. In this image, what is the dominant value being addressed? What other needs or values might be part of this food presentation?

◎ VALUE IN ARTISTIC DINING

The styles, and thus their menus, reflect changes in peoples' attitudes about eating. What constitutes a meal changes not only what is eaten but also how what is eaten looks. The look of food changes for different price points and styles of services in all sectors of Professional cuisine. Changes in food design could be developed for any sector in the hospitality industry, but as the price of a meal goes up, the look of plated food is increasingly emphasized. Until very recently, there was a very clear hierarchy in the way food trends developed—they spread from the most expensive, formal restaurants out across other areas. In recent years, there is evidence of artistic dining being inspired by trends not only from home-style cooking, but also in fast-food and industrially manufactured foods.

The archetypal plate designs relate to artistic dining when it is assumed that the aesthetic experience is an important reason for such dining. That is not to say that the ingredients will not be chosen to meet the chef's standards about sustainability or to offer vegetarian options for the diners, but the emphasis goes beyond those considerations in stylizing the look of those choices. The ingredients and *dishes* used to create such plates must also, to some degree, satisfy hunger and provide nourishment, but diners want more than a substantial meal; they want a dining experience.

Why diners are willing to pay for a more expensive dining experience cannot be explained by one simple answer. However, the expectations of such customers are reflected in the change of labeling for this type of dining from *fine* to *artistic*.

Initially, one of the central reasons people went to an expensive restaurant was a social display that marked a distinction of class. The wealthy class of society set cultural styles in fashion, art, and leisure that filtered down and were emulated in less expensive versions. People who did not have enough money to live in the style of the rich and famous would go to a fine dining restaurant to mark a special occasion or gain a window into such exclusivity. People displayed "good taste" by dining finely in contrast to common or popular qualities of food. (OED 2011, fine) Some words associated with the description of "good" or "fine taste" are:

Superior   **Refined**   subtle   **Rare**   Formal   **Excellent**   **Distinguished**

Quality   **Elegant**   **Luxurious**   Elaborate   *Delicate*   **Beautiful**

As society became more democratic, fine dining, although still referred to as such, was also referred to as destination dining, implying less an idea of exclusivity and more an idea of specialness that was worth experiencing. The experience was something out of the ordinary that could provide not only pleasure but expanded understanding. Dining could be a way of learning, a type of connoisseurship. It broadened one's horizons by providing experiences that had to be considered to be appreciated. So while all the qualities listed above were still applicable to destination dining, words that described a customer's viewpoint became important in the definition of this type of dining; for example:

Aware   Knowledgeable   Gourmet   **Appreciative**   Informed

It was assumed that the chefs preparing this food were experts, and that through experience and reflection, customers would develop an understanding of not only quality ingredients and flavor pairings but also different chefs' styles. Beginning with the Nouvelle style, food might be any of the qualities listed for "fine" dining but it might also be described as:

Simple purity   Authentic   Casual elegance   **Remarkable**

Fine dining, that is to say *destination dining,* has also more recently been labeled *artistic dining*. This shift reflects a change in aesthetic value which suggests that to appreciate something does not necessitate a cultivation of understanding but rather an intuitive or emotional response provoked by an experience. The type of words used to describe artistic dining build on all the previous aspects, adding qualities such as:

Clever   Surprising   Unusual   Conceptual   **Original**
Complicated   **Appealing**   Contrived

Throughout all these changes in high-end dining, the approach taken by all the chefs working in this type of establishment is **playful sophistication**. It is the ability to take a vast sum of previous knowledge about what food means in many different settings, and, through expert technique, create an engaging meal.

FIGURE 13.4

Describing Beauty.
What words would you use to describe the artful presentation in this image?

The importance of noticing such shifts in meaning in expensive dining is the perspective it provides. The changes in artistic food values represent aesthetic cultural shifts for both chefs and customers. When you look at a presentation, some of the many words listed above are better at describing the effect achieved; with such words, you can better decide if a plate matches the tone of the menu for a specific occasion or establishment.

The term artistic dining, as it relates to the customers, is relatively new, but the term *artistic cooking* has been in use since at least the late 1800s. Originally, it was synonymous with ornamental or decorative cookery. This type of cookery was associated with the displays of food made during the Table Frame, where highly elaborate socles elevated dishes such as *Bastion en Pain de Foie à la Mazagran* (see color inset Images 2, 4, 5). These presentations reflect the older values of the Table Frame created through figurative shaping of foods and complicated embellishments (Dubois 1856, 390).

Even in 1893, Chef Jessup Whitehead, wrote in *Cooking for Profit—A New American Cookbook*:

> **"Still, as 'BEAUTY IS ITS OWN EXCUSE FOR BEING,' we must pursue the
> ornamental branches as a labor of love, because we take pleasure
> in showing such work, as the cooks of the largest cities yearly make
> displays of pieces that cost them nights and days of patient toil,
> simply keeping up the fashions of other times for their own pride and
> gratification" (Whitehead 1893, 178).**

The pride and gratification that Chef Whitehead is referring to is central to all chefs and cooks, but it is taken to the extreme in artistic dining; such beliefs are at the core of craft endeavors, where work is done well for its own sake. It is true that all cooks and chefs must make money, but for an artisan, the work itself is the primary motivation; the rest follows. Artistic, or destination, or fine dining kitchens must achieve the most exacting standards of our profession; this is one of the principal reasons a cook or chef chooses to work in such an establishment. This exactitude of craft combined with the scope of creativity in such kitchens provides tremendous fulfillment.

◎ VALUES IN PROFESSIONAL TRAINING

How a person learns to cook is based on a system extrapolated from a vast body of previous work that grew from a common source of methodology. Methodology is a system of thinking that outlines the way a task is to be done within a field of study or research; it is an approach to formulating questions and the methods used to find the answers. For example, the scientific method consists of observing, hypothesizing, experimenting, analyzing, and evaluating.

Throughout this book, plated presentations have been considered as a design process, but it must be remembered that this process is happening within the larger context of craft. Traditionally, design was part of all crafts' methodology; as society became more industrial and specialized, product design became a specialization. Designers now are rarely the people who make the products they design; rather, they create prototypes. Thus, there is a distance between the designer, the production workers, and the customers.

A chef's methodology relies on a more immediate connection with the materials of the production—ingredients—and on a more intimate service of customers. As a craft methodology, culinary art is collaborative; it combines the understandings gained from intimately working with food with methods used in business, science, and art. These fields, in turn, have developed methods specific to their desired results, and, oftentimes, experts in these fields rely on chefs to bring their specific type of knowledge to projects. The special viewpoint that a chef brings to such projects is a deep understanding of working with food and customers; the cultivation of this insight is the reason a chef is capable of seeing many different layers of meaning on a plate. This is the special sight of a chef.

The methodologies of science, business, art, and design have different relationships with food. These all come together in the craft of culinary art. Although at times chefs might emphasize one method of working with food, culinary art requires a binding of all these types of knowledge to express flavor. Practice and repetition provide the technical ability fundamental to all culinary expressions. A practiced chef, before even tasting the food, can see flavor in shape, texture, color, amount, temperature, pattern, space, proportion, height, composition, and harmony or contrast of foods.

The chef's sight is developed through a cook's hands. It is the result of years of touching and tasting food that build a physical connection with ingredients as well as the connection that results from participating in a tradition. Meaning is transmitted through repertoires passed from master cook to beginning cook, creating a living history of eating. A cook develops a deep connection to these professional traditions and to nature through her work, and the result of her work is a physical reality that connects to a waiting customer. As culinary studies become more inclusive of global food traditions, and culinary work becomes more fragmented into specialized fields such as product development and nutritional analysis, the holistic craft approach to culinary understanding risks becoming marginalized. This is why it is important that theories describing culinary work come from within the professional kitchen.

These types of considerations do not take place within a working kitchen, nor should they. Furthermore, successful chefs might never deliberately contemplate ideas about culinary aesthetics or ethics; instead, they are deeply embedded in their unspoken practice. In fact, too much theoretical thought can be a stumbling block to creative work. Yet, there are times when reflecting on practice can make it stronger: principally, at the beginning of a career, and, later after some years of working.

At the beginning of a career, it is important because it helps a cook understand what she is seeing more experienced chefs do, and it helps a beginning cook choose more carefully what chef or area of food service her values are more closely aligned with. Later, after years of practice, articulated reflection can help transmit understanding more easily to younger practitioners so that what forms the "cooking-self" is passed along in formalized learning, such as a structured apprenticeship program or within a culinary school.

In between these two periods are the working years, which allow limited time for contemplation. These are the years when it is sufficient to "live the questions." Rainer Maria Rilke, an established poet of the early 1900s, gave this advice when asked how to prosper as a poet:

> *. . . . have patience with everything unresolved in your heart and to try to love the questions themselves as if they were locked rooms or books written in a very foreign language. Don't search for the answers, which could not be given to you now, because you would not be able to live them. And the point is to live everything. Live the questions now. Perhaps then, someday far in the future, you will gradually, without even noticing it, live your way into the answer (Rilke 1934, 34–35).*

During the years of duplicating presentations and repetitive kitchen work, unnoticed theory is being learned. A beginning practitioner is doing more than learning to cook; she is developing a chef's sight. The professional chef's way of looking translates foods' visual forms into mind flavors, or, conversely, visualizes flavor concepts into physical forms and patterns, but it is through the doing that the ability to see is learned.

◎ WRAPPING UP

When artist Paul Cezanne said, "The day is coming when a single carrot, freshly observed, will set off a revolution," he was not talking about food but a way of looking at the world. For a chef, the quotation works at both levels. When a chef looks at a carrot and decides how to use it, she is defining her vision of how humanity fits in the food chain of world; also, when she presents said carrot, she is visually exposing her culinary values. She is giving physical form to not only her theory of culinary aesthetics but also her beliefs about culinary ethics (Gasquet 1991, 68).

Food images, from those on the Web to those in cookbooks, affect what people think "good" food looks like. Cooks and chefs must take time to consider this effect in light of what they know to be true about cooking because images have a way of seducing the eye. Food that is to be photographed is often styled, but the same food, cooked to be eaten, often does not look the same. If you cook food to the image of food, it will taste different.

As plating is used more to create *dishes*, understanding what makes food enjoyable has to be considered; culinary thought did not need to be so rigorous when creativity was not as important as an established repertoire. Yet, from the earliest occasions when we remember eating, *dishes* are the building blocks used to understand food. What *dishes* have been served at holidays and everyday meals preface our later professional ideas. By establishing a repertoire, a chef adds her personal history of food traditions to that of a diverse professional community.

Because chefs are now all working in different styles and coming from these diverse backgrounds, a common understanding of food can no longer be assumed within the profession. For this reason, practitioners must articulate the theories that underlie their assumptions of what food is or should be. The chef of today requires not only the fundamentals of any one cuisine, but a method to relate cuisines through professional theory.

By *framing* Professional cuisine within the parameters of service method and menu structure, all areas of food service can be investigated and analyzed as they relate to working practice. It becomes possible to not only appreciate what has been done but also use the knowledge to inform contemporary decisions. The *culinary Art history* is an aid in understanding why there are different beliefs about food presentation. Using the style's guidelines within the Plate Frame, cooks and chefs can analyze their own work and better understand the work of others.

Considering the meanings of visual food leads to a deeper understanding of a chef's practice. The ways food is presented are signals that hopefully match our customers' expectations. Ultimately, beyond the ability to manipulate ingredients into prescribed results, what we are trying to do, through our practice, is answer two questions that define our industry:

In the choices I make about ingredients and cooking processes, what am I promoting as **Food**? And, what values are expressed by the style of **Service**? In other words, what and why do I think people should eat? And, what values are being presented as important, such as convenience or nourishment?

QUERIES & INQUIRIES

1. Consider one of your favorite ingredients, such as a type of cheese. Now list all the elaborations you could do with the ingredient.

   For example, I have this most excellent goat cheese, which I am thrilled to eat chunks of. I could bread it, fry it, and serve it on top of a salad; or, I could use as it a filling in ravioli; or, I could melt it into a cheese sauce. Now, if I decide on any of these elaborations, I need to ask myself: Did I better highlight the goodness of the cheese? Or, would this cheese have best been served simply, by itself, with grilled bread?

   a. Answer these questions in relation to the ingredient you chose.

   b. The larger questions are: Why do we elaborate an ingredient? And, if we do elaborate an ingredient, what are we trying to achieve?

2. Consider the customer values described in this chapter. How might a chef respond to meet the values? Describe how food presentation might be affected.

- ◆ Satiation
- ◆ Nourishment
- ◆ Convenience
- ◆ Sociability
- ◆ Celebration
- ◆ Exploration
- ◆ Ethical considerations

3. Describe culinary methodology. How does it relate to the special sight of a chef?

4. There are four images in this chapter. Can you see what values are emphasized by the presentations?

CITATION AND REFERENCE MATERIALS

Archer, Bruce, Baynes, Ken, and Roberts, Phil. *The Nature of Research into Design and Technology Education.* Leicestershire, UK: IDATER99, Loughborough University, 2001. Institutional Repository: Item 2134/1687. 1992. Retrieved November 12, 2006, at hdl.hasndle.net/2134/1687.

Archer, Bruce. *The Nature of Research in Design and Design Education.* 1991. idater.lboro.ac.uk/the-nature-of-research-into-design-and-design-education.

Friedman, Ken. Keynote Addresses from IDATER99 and IDATER2000: *Creating Design Knowledge: From Research into Practice.*

Dubois, Urbain, and Bernard, Emile. *La Cuisine Classique études pratiques, raisonnées et de l'école Française appli-qué au service a la russe.* Paris: Chez Les Auteurs, 1856. University of Washington Libraries, p. 390, plate 97.

"fine, adj., n.2, and adv."12d. 13b. OED Online (March 2011). Oxford University Press. Retrieved April 23, 2011, at www.oed.com/view/Entry/70361?rskey=YePDZB&result=3.

Gasquet, Joachim. Artist quote from *Cezanne, a Memoir with Conversations*, "What I Know or Have Seen of His Life." English edition. London: Thames and Hudson, 1991.

Jessup, Whitehead. *Cooking for Profit, a New American Cookbook Adapted for the Use of All Who Serve Meals for a Price.* Massachusetts: Applewood Books. Originally published in 1893.

Maslow, Abraham H. *Motivation and Personality.* 3rd ed. New York: Harper & Row, Inc., 1987.

Rilke, Rainer Maria. *Letters to a Young Poet.* Norton, Herter M.D. translator. Revised edition. New York: W.W. Norton & Company, 1934, pp. 34–35.

Risatti, Howard. *A Theory of Craft.* Chapel Hill: The University of North Carolina Press, 2007.

Roberts, Phil. "An Invitation to IDATER99." In E. W. L. Norman and P. H. Roberts, ed. *Design and Technology Educational Research and Curriculum Development: The Emerging International Research Agenda.* Leicestershire, UK: IDATER99, Loughborough University, 2001.

Schon, Donald A. *The Reflective Practitioner: How Professionals Think in Action.* New York: Basic Books, 1983.

GLOSSARY

The number that appears after the term refers to the chapter in which the word or phrase is discussed.

Amuse-bouche (7): Literally meaning "mouth amuser," these tiny bites are offered at the discretion of the chef, just after the diner orders—they are not part of the order.

Artistic dining (6): See entry for fine dining.

Axiology, culinary (1): A type of study that considers the criteria applied in determining "value"; the philosophy of aesthetics and the principles of ethics are formal areas of study in axiology. Culinary axiology is the study of why we find certain presentations beautiful, and why we may consider certain food choices to be good.

BUFF plate design (6): A plate design beginning in New American style, generally using the standard combination of meat, starch, and vegetable, which are centered in the middle of the plate. The acronym stands for balance, unity, focal point, and flow.

California cuisine (6): Really part of the New American style of Professional cuisine, this term was used by media to highlight the important developments happening in California restaurants during the 1970s and 1980s. Grilling was the predominant cooking method. Pizzas and salads rose to main course status with the use of unexpected ingredients. Local ingredients, often organic, were highlighted with Asian and Mediterranean influences. The presentations were, in general, much less elaborate than in Nouvelle dishes. These developments were labeled in the press as casual "fine" dining and contemporary American "cuisine."

Classical style (4): A style of Professional cuisine, symbolized by Chef August Escoffier. Established tenets exist for the pairing of foods and the naming of dishes. Classical dishes are generally served using Russian- or French-style service. This style was most widely used during the Platter Frame.

Course within a Course plate design (7): A plate design beginning in the Global style; these presentations, like the Elemental and Duo/Trio designs, present individual dishes with considerable empty space between them. The difference is that, in this design, the dishes are placed in an order best eaten, like sequencing courses of a menu.

culinary Art history (3): An organizational system, emphasizing the craft of cooking underlying the art of food design, developed to contextualize changing styles of food presentations.

culinary Art history **Frame** (3): Periods defined by service style and menu structure can be understood as Frames, which create boundaries for the presentation of foods. In this history, there are four Frames; three Frames, reflecting periods prior to the current Plate Frame, influenced artistic dining in the United States. These early Frames are found in the dining customs and manners of the European nobility. In contrast, styles within the later Plate Frame, where the presentation boundaries are set by the plate, are more diverse.

Culinary constructionism (8): Using the isolated compounds found in foods by scientists, chefs reassemble different foods constructing new flavors or textures.

Culinary context (2): The setting for which a dish is designed; it is based on the parameters of food category, price point, and service style.

Culinary repertoire (2): The range of dishes and techniques that a cook can execute well. The cooking knowledge a cook or chef can demonstrate from memory.

Deconstruction/Abstraction (7): A plate design beginning in the Global style; ingredients are presented in random patterns but when eaten form a complete dish.

Destination dining (13): See entry for fine dining.

Dish/plate (2): These words are often used interchangeably; however, in this book they are used to represent two different concepts. A plate is a piece of serviceware without any food on it. A dish is the combination of foods and ingredients to create flavors.

Duos/trios plate design (6): A plate design beginning in the New American style; a focus food is presented in multiple ways on the same plate.

Elemental plate design (6): A plate design beginning in the Fusion style; separate dishes are served on the same plate with considerable empty space between them.

English-style service (3): Wait staff present platters to diners and serve them from the platters, acting in place of the table's host.

Entrée (3): During the Table Frame, entrées were a category of dishes served during the first course. They were often poultry or smaller meat dishes, such as lamb chops. During service à la russe, they are generally the third or fourth course in a menu, to be followed by large roasts. In the United States, this term has come to mean the main course, while for contemporary European menus, the term has come to signify a beginning course.

Entremets (3): During the Room Frame, entremets were elaborate food displays, often figurative, that were carried into the room between the serving of foods. During the Table Frame, using service à la française, these dishes were part of second table; entremets included hot sweet dishes and important vegetable dishes. Using service à la russe, during the Platter Frame, this term came to represent the dessert course.

Face plate design (4): This is the most straightforward method of plating a meat, one starch, and one vegetable. It is used in a wide range of applications from a diner's special to a wait-staff–plated Classical dish.

Fan plate design (5): A plate design beginning in the Nouvelle style; the vegetables and starches radiate from the top of the focus food.

Figurative food (3): Foods that are shaped to resemble a building, animal, or person.

Fine dining (2): This traditional term is not the best name for this type of eating experience today. Instead, this type of dining experience is better referred to as artistic or destination dining. While this type of restaurant still requires a certain economic status, the reasons people choose to dine there are less about class delineation and more about experiencing an artful perspective of considered cooking. Artistic dining is the most formalized dining experience, and as such, generates the most criteria about plate presentations.

Food category (2): This term is drawn from the function a food is intended for, such as breakfast, lunch, dinner, snack, or passed appetizers.

Friandises (4): Small, one-bite iced cakes; a type of petit four served, generally with coffee, at the end of the meal.

Fusion style (6): A style of Professional cuisine in the Plate Frame. This style created dishes by fusing together techniques, dishes, and ingredients from two distinct traditional geographical cuisines. The plate design that was often used at the beginning of this style was Elemental, but other designs from the New American style are also used.

Gastronome (12): A person, much like a gourmet or connoisseur, who cultivates understanding about food and drink but also goes on to write about her opinions.

Gastronomy (12): A field of knowledge centered on eating. It is an umbrella term that combines food understandings through many disciplines such as history, science, aesthetics, and physiology. The word implies considered eating, refinement—not simply consumption.

Givrés (10): A frozen dessert in which fruit is scooped out to create cups; the pulp is then turned into a sorbet and replaced in the fruit cups.

Global style (7): A style of Professional cuisine in the Plate Frame; plate designs in this style focus on the individual characteristics of ingredients. The plate designs often used in this style are Linear, Course within a Course, and Deconstruction / Abstraction.

Gourmet (12): A connoisseur; such a person develops the palate to be sensitive to the subtleties of food and drink. Connoisseurs are considered to be experts in matters of taste as a result of their extensive knowledge.

Grande cuisine (4): A term used to describe the elaborate cooking done in aristocratic and royal households by professional chefs. This term is not used in the framework of the culinary Art history, as it implies there are multiple cuisines, instead of one Professional cuisine with many styles.

Hâtelet (3): Decorative skewers used to garnish some dishes generally found in the Platter Frame. Assembled like a shish-kabob, these skewers are filled with ornamental, luxury foods, such as whole truffles, and then are stuck into a food presentation.

Haute cuisine (4): A term used to describe the cooking done by professional chefs in fine dining. This term is not used in the framework of the culinary Art history, as it implies there are multiple cuisines, instead of one Professional cuisine with many styles.

Illusion food (3): Foods that look like a well-known dish but are made of an unexpected ingredient.

Island(s) plate design (5): A plate design beginning in the Nouvelle style; focus foods are surrounded by sauce and topped with a garnish.

Linear plate design (7): A plate design beginning in the Global style; these presentations are generally presented on square or rectangular plates. The foods are placed along lines of an imaginary grid.

Menu format (2): The format of a menu is a synergy of food category and service style. The format shapes what decisions the customer can make in food choices; examples are à la carte, special event, tasting menu, and cycle.

Mignardises (4): Various types of petit fours, which are small, bite-size sweets, such as tiny cookies and cakes served, generally with coffee, at the end of the meal.

Millefeuille (5): Typically a dessert, sometimes called a Napoleon, consisting of three layers of puff pastry and two layers of flavored whipped cream.

Molecular gastronomy (8): A scientific field focused on culinary preparations.

Mound plate design (6): A plate design beginning in the New American style; there is not one focus food but, rather, a careful arrangement of bite-size foods.

New American style (6): A style of Professional cuisine in the Plate Frame that grew out of the increasing ability and confidence of American chefs to expand beyond European traditions. They blended diverse backgrounds, iconic American dishes, and the bounty of American food markets. The plate designs often used in this style are Duos /Trios, the Stack, the Mound, and BUFF.

Nouvelle style (5): A style of Professional cuisine in the Plate Frame. Originally defined by ten guiding criteria, this style focuses on less manipulation of ingredients and creativity compared to the Classical style. The plate designs often used in this style are the Sun, the Sun-bug, the Fan, and Island(s).

Plate archetypes (9): Models of plate designs often associated with certain shifts in the craft of cooking.

Plate Frame (5): A style period of the *culinary Art history* in which cooks and chefs arrange the food on plates in the kitchen. There are many different professional presentation styles within this Frame.

Plating (2): The arrangement of dishes and/or ingredients on a plate; it focuses on the look of presented dishes. Plating uses food ingredients, or dishes, already cooked or structured and arranges them on serviceware.

Platter Frame (3): A pre-plate style period of the *culinary Art history,* created in large part by the development of *service à la russe* and accompanying menus in which food was sequenced into a single dish per course, the same for each diner. The early sequences of à la carte menus use some elements of this Frame, with wait staff moving food onto plates in the dining room.

Professional cuisine (1): A body of knowledge created by chefs, past and present, that defines the way meals are sequenced, foods are valued, flavors are paired, and cooking processes are used in professional kitchens. Essential to Professional cuisine is the principle that plating is dependent on menu structure and service style.

Relevé (3): A category of dishes developed during the Table Frame. These dishes, during a *service à la française*, replace soup and fish dishes on the table. They were often smaller meat dishes in a sauce. During *service à la russe,* relevés come before the category of dishes called entrées in the menu.

Room Frame (3): The earliest style period in the *culinary Art history* discussed in this manual; presentations were designed to be paraded into a room. Feather wrapped roasted peacocks and swans are examples of presentations from this period. Figurative foods and illusion foods were popular.

Satiety value (2): The amount that a certain ingredient, food, or dish is perceived to be filling. It often relates to the amount of fat or carbohydrate present. It is often described by such phrases as a heavy meal or a light dish.

Service à la carte (3): Restaurant customers order from a menu. Not all the diners at the table eat the same dishes, or even the same menu courses. This service style is also referred to as American service or individual plate service.

Service à la française (French-style service) (3): Originally used during the Table Frame, this type of service was like an elaborate family-style meal where all the foods are placed on the table and diners help themselves to whatever is in polite reach. Contemporary meaning varies among professionals, as this style of service uses elements from Russian-style service, English-style service, and American-style service. Wait staff may prepare some courses from a service trolley, present other courses on platters that they serve from, or bring completed dishes from the kitchen.

Service à la russe (Russian-style service) (3): Originally used during the transitional Platter Frame, this type of service required a server to present and serve guests from platters brought in a sequence to the table. Contemporary meaning can vary among professionals to encompass not only serving from platters but also serving from a service trolley.

Service au Guéridon (Guéridon service) (3): This style of service, in which wait staff work from service-trolleys, is often considered synonymous with *service à la russe*. Yet, this term may be used to sidestep any confusion between exactly which style of service is being used by describing the method: service from trolleys in the dining room.

Service style (2): The method in which food is delivered to a customer; examples of service styles include plated, family style, banquet, buffet, cafeteria, carry-out, and packaged.

Socle (3): A supporting base for foods made of edible materials that add height, and embellishment, to a dish.

Spa cuisine (5): Really, another style of Professional cuisine, not a separate cuisine; this style developed alongside Nouvelle style. It shares the philosophy of lightening sauces, decreasing portion size, and focusing on fresh, simply cooked ingredients. The point was to prepare healthful, low-calorie dishes that would please a sophisticated palate.

Stack plate design (6): A plate design beginning in the New American style; the focus food, vegetables, and starch are layered on top of each other.

Sun plate design (5): One of the earliest plate designs by chefs plating in the kitchen; it was first used during the Nouvelle style of Professional cuisine. Accompaniments to the focus food radiate around the outside of the plate.

Table Frame (3): A pre-plate style period of the *culinary Art history* in which a course, or service, was defined by a table plan. *Service à la française* defines this period, which highlighted sophisticated, refined, ordered presentations.

Techno-emotive style (8): A style of Professional cuisine that uses the knowledge of molecular gastronomy to design dishes. This style is also sometimes referred to as avant-garde, modern, or alchemic.

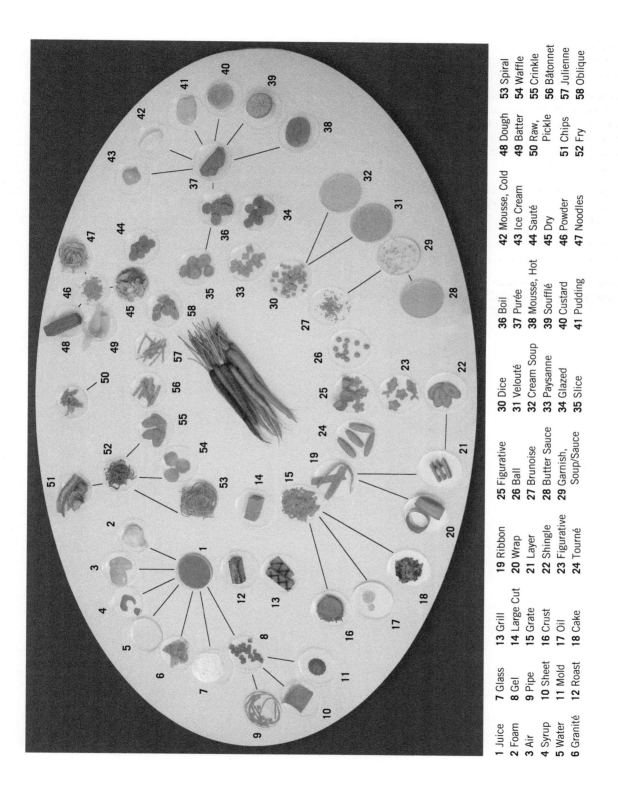

1 Juice
2 Foam
3 Air
4 Syrup
5 Water
6 Granité
7 Glass
8 Gel
9 Pipe
10 Sheet
11 Mold
12 Roast
13 Grill
14 Large Cut
15 Grate
16 Crust
17 Oil
18 Cake
19 Ribbon
20 Wrap
21 Layer
22 Shingle
23 Figurative
24 Tourné
25 Figurative
26 Ball
27 Brunoise
28 Butter Sauce
29 Garnish,
   Soup/Sauce
30 Dice
31 Velouté
32 Cream Soup
33 Paysanne
34 Glazed
35 Slice
36 Boil
37 Purée
38 Mousse, Hot
39 Soufflé
40 Custard
41 Pudding
42 Mousse, Cold
43 Ice Cream
44 Sauté
45 Dry
46 Powder
47 Noodles
48 Dough
49 Batter
50 Raw,
   Pickle
51 Chips
52 Fry
53 Spiral
54 Waffle
55 Crinkle
56 Bâtonnet
57 Julienne
58 Oblique

INDEX